# EKARACH CHANDON

THE MOST CHALLENGING STORY TO PEN DOWN
IS THE ONE THAT BEAUTIFIES OUR HEARTS.

BECAUSE WHEN IT COMES TO PEOPLE, THEY'RE SO
INTIMATELY CLOSE THAT NO INVENTION FROM ANY
HUMAN ERA CAN BRIDGE THE DISTANCE.

LET'S EMBARK ON THIS JOURNEY TOGETHER, TO
UNVEIL THE MYSTERY THAT EACH ONE OF US HARBORS.

THIS EXPEDITION WILL LIKELY LEAD US TO UNCOVER
THE SECRETS OF HUMANITY, AND GRANT US THE
ABILITY TO INSCRIBE OUR HEARTS BEAUTIFULLY,
ALIGNING WITH OUR TRUE DESIRES.

# 'HUMAN' SECRET

IT'S TIME TO DISCERN HOW WE AND THE UNIVERSE ARE INTRICATELY CONNECTED.

TRUTH 2 OF 5 : TRUTH FROM NEW THOUGHT

# 'HUMAN'

---

THE INTIMATE STORY

WE SHOULD BE LEARNING TO KNOW

BEFORE WE BECOME...

STRANGERS TO OURSELVES ....

FOR EVERY EXPLORER AND SEEKER

WITHOUT EXPLORERS,

THERE'S NO PATH FOR THE NEXT GENERATION,

AND WITHOUT THOSE IN SEARCH,

JOURNEYS MERELY BECOME LEGENDS.

.....

"HUMAN SECRET" EKARACH CHANDON

"IF WE WRITE BOOKS WITH A DEEP SENSE OF
RESPONSIBILITY, BELIEVING THAT THE BOOK IS
WRITTEN FOR OUR FUTURE SELVES TO READ IN
THE NEXT LIFE, THEN PERHAPS THERE WOULD
BE FEWER FALSEHOODS IN THE WORLD.

AND IF THE KNOWLEDGE CREATED WITHIN HUMAN
CIVILIZATION WAS SUCH THAT ITS CREATOR COULD
HONESTLY ANSWER WHY IT WAS CONCEIVED, THEN
THE CULTURE SHAPED BY THIS KNOWLEDGE WOULD
NOT LEAD HUMANITY ASTRAY."

"HUMAN SECRET" EKARACH CHANDON

# ABOUT THIS BOOK

This book was initially written on May 1, 2007, and completed on May 14, 2007. The author, overwhelmed by a compulsion to write, penned down his insights and observations.

At a time when the world is rife with numerous challenges,If we consider the root cause of many major problems, often they can be traced back to human, just one 'human'.

The chaos that ensues stems from our lack of self-awareness. If the human psyche were no longer a secret, the myriad problems we encounter in the world, in our societies, and within ourselves might eventually diminish. ...

"HUMAN SECRET" EKARACH CHANDON

# ABOUT THE AUTHOR BEHIND "HUMAN SECRET"

The Conscientious Responsibility for a society where individuals truly understand themselves is deeply rooted in the author's heart. He yearns for a society that exists in serenity and contentment, one that thrives without pulling its members astray, losing their path. The author believes that there are many who share this vision for a society that exists in serenity and contented happiness.

Yet, observing the realities of our world today, countless issues seem to hinder us from even getting to know ourselves. If we don't truly know who we are, how can we navigate life without losing our way?

With a firm belief that everyone has the capacity for introspection and recognizes their own worth, this book was penned down.

"HUMAN SECRET" EKARACH CHANDON

# ACKNOWLEDGEMENTS

Thank you to everyone who has enlightened me about the nature of humans. I'm grateful for all the events and experiences that have deepened my understanding.

I hope this book serves as a token of appreciation for the knowledge I have gained from each one of you.

My wish is for the essence of humanity to no longer remain a mystery to us.

With heartfelt thanks,
...

"HUMAN SECRET" EKARACH CHANDON

# WHY I WROTE THIS BOOK

Before I put pen to paper,
I always ask myself why am I writing this?
What value does this writing, "Human Secret," hold for
its readers?

The Responsibility behind this book can be illuminated
by the following story:

I once visited a school for the blind,
accompanied by a colleague who works in
education. We brought sighted children to meet
those without sight.

Before the visit, as part of an experiment, *I tried
living while blindfolded for several days, spending many
hours each day without the ability to see. However,* **I
was only able to do a little.**

I realized that these children possessed
something more profound than those with
vision. Just by closing our eyes and
experiencing life for a single day, the profound
challenges become evident, making life almost
unbearable.

**"HUMAN SECRET" EKARACH CHANDON**

Yet, what I observed in those blind children was a stronger zest for life compared to many sighted individuals. A determination to live life fully, despite their physical limitations.

Their spirit moved me so much that I felt compelled to relay a message to the sighted: "Live life like you truly are alive, utilize your capabilities as if you have a heart beating passionately within."

Best wishes,
Uncle Mai Jaidi

**"Live life like you truly are alive, utilize your capabilities as if you still have a heart inside you"**

This sentiment alone encapsulates the entire reason I wrote this book.

With Conscientious Responsibility,
Ekarach Chandon

"HUMAN SECRET" EKARACH CHANDON

To all the goodness born from the creation and transmission of knowledge in these books, I dedicate to Unyanee Mooksombud, my dearly beloved wife and the ultimate treasure of my life and heart. Her presence has shown me that in life's every choice, nothing is more significant or precious than love.

Though her physical form may have departed, in love, she remains eternal.

For any mistakes that have arisen in conveying knowledge within these pages, I alone bear responsibility.

**EKARACH CHANDON**

# TABLE OF CONTENTS

"HUMAN" SECRET

**EKARACH CHANDON**

# TABLE OF CONTENTS

"HUMAN"

SECRET

**EKARACH CHANDON**

# TABLE OF CONTENTS

EKARACH CHANDON

"WHEN WE KNOW ONE
TRUTH, WE HAVE
ABILITY TO KNOW ALL
THE TRUTHS."

Ekarach Chandon
Truth Quote 2005

Secret 1st: The Secret of the Universe

"HUMAN SECRET"

# Secret 1st: The Secret of the Universe

*Why Bother Knowing About 'Human'?*

This narrative Uncle is about to share gives us a brief glimpse into *the human enigma.* It delves into the mysteries of the universe and is a continuation of the story *"Read Before the Meaning of Your Life is Lesser,"* which Uncle previously shared with us. Uncle suggests we **fully comprehend** the introduction before delving into the content.

*"Why do we endeavor to learn about humans?"*
Contrary to the above question, Uncle ponders another:
*"Why not endeavor learn to know about humans?"*

In his extensive reading, Uncle rarely found material that offered **deeper insight** into our own being. Despite this, *understanding ourselves* remains a paramount aspect of life.

There's likely no need for Uncle to elaborate on its significance. After all, **without humans**, it's not just that we wouldn't know life, but there would be **no life to cherish and live.**

# Secret 1st: The Secret of the Universe

*In the realm of work,* knowledge is paramount.
*In the pursuit of happiness,* understanding life is crucial.

Isn't it our **lack of understanding** in life that renders our passing days **devoid of joy and meaning?**

Before embarking on this journey through the book, Uncle poses a **reflective question** for us to ponder: **The foremost question before setting forth:**

*What do we seek in this transient life?*
Is it the **enduring joy** in one's heart or ...
...**mere fleeting pleasures day by day?**

If it's the **lasting happiness** that resonates within, then let us continue on **this journey together.**

So, where shall we journey next? Through this tale, Uncle will likely introduce us to the concept of **'human.'**

*Why the emphasis on understanding 'human',*
you may wonder?

# Secret 1st: The Secret of the Universe

**For Uncle, comprehending humanity unlocks an all-encompassing understanding.** Because, from Uncle's perspective, the universe is mirrored thusly.

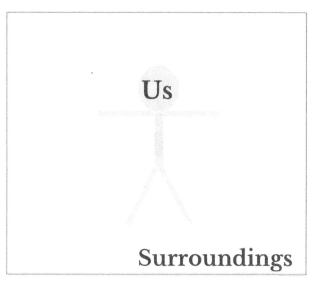

*Picture 1. New thought ; Conceptual of the universe*

*At this point, Uncle isn't sure what to call it. Uncle would like to "define" it as the 'universe' for now. It consists of two parts: us and the surroundings.*

# Secret 1st: The Secret of the Universe

Let me explain again the general outline of the universe that I see. As Uncle has determined, it is also called.

The universe: The *"Universal Image"* or the *"Cosmic Data Blueprint"*. This could be perceived as the data field that determines the overall format of what we recognize as the "universe", or the general data structure within which we reside. A simple question to understand the existence of this phenomenon: How does a vast structure like the universe, which houses our very existence, manage such enormous, intricate data?

Us: *"Us"* or *"Inner Data Being"*. This pertains to the data that's associated with our very essence, inclusive of our thoughts, feelings, and everything that transpires within us – "Rûŝụk", "Khid", "Rû". The scope and magnitude of this is ever-changing, evolving in line with our "Kileš".

In terms of our "Kileš", those wishing to study without getting overwhelmed by "others' knowledge, "The knowledge of others is just our data." Uncle recommends starting by reading, questioning, and responding to the book, *Read Before the Meaning of Your Life is Lesser.*

# Secret 1st: The Secret of the Universe

**Environment:** *"Surroundings"* or *"External Data Surroundings"*. This involves data from outside, or the environment we interact with, along with general information from the world and the universe.

It correlates with our Inner Data Being. One can observe this data if they start recognizing their "S̄ìng thī̀ rū̂s̄ụk" promptly.

For a deeper dive into this topic, consider reading "Truth from New Thought", specifically volume 1 titled *Read Before the Meaning of Your Life is Lesser.*

**Regarding our relationship with the universe** and how data operates, Uncle will elaborate on this in detail in the future.

For the specialized terms used in this book, readers can gain understanding from the book *"Read Before the Meaning of Your Life is Lesser".*

# Secret 1st: The Secret of the Universe

**What I've explained so far** represents the universal perspective I hold. This section is crucial, and I intend to delineate it in greater detail in an upcoming book. However, in studying the *"Secrets of Humanity"* from this fresh cosmic viewpoint, as previously emphasized, there's an even more pivotal matter for the content of this book: the organization of information for our easier comprehension and self-study.

This can be deliberated as follows:

Considering the two aspects, if our goal is to comprehend the universe's truth, which approach would we select between:

**Approach 1:** *Study the entire environment.* Once we understand everything about the environment, what remains is us. Thus, we will know everything.

**Approach 2:** *Begin by understanding ourselves.* Once we truly know who we are, anything that isn't us is the environment. Thus, we will know everything.

*Which method might be more time-efficient and simpler for studying?*

# Secret 1st: The Secret of the Universe

Which method would be more time-efficient and straightforward in our studies?

Give it a thought.
For Uncle, *I choose to study ourselves first.* It's shorter, closer, and Uncle doesn't need to learn things that are yet unnecessary.

Because if we truly recognize ourselves,
Anything we touch or interact with that isn't us becomes our environment.
Then, we'd know everything.

The things we interact with,
We only need to know as much as it concerns us.

**Once we know one thing, we know it all.**
**That one thing? It's us.**

To clearly understand the boundaries of ourselves, one must keenly assess the point where we intersect with our surroundings, separating it from us. The environment Uncle speaks of isn't merely the air that surrounds us.

# Secret 1st: The Secret of the Universe

It's everything that affects us: words, thoughts, actions, how others feel about us, or even the perceptions we construct from our own prejudices.

Once we discern these prejudices clearly and separate them, Uncle solely calls them our 'environment'.

If we perceive and understand the environment in this manner, then we would also comprehend the suffering that occurs due to the co-existence of us and our environment. Because we can't distinctly segregate ourselves from it, the repercussions of the environment thus affect us.

If seen lucidly, we wouldn't tread into areas where the environment is harmful, **potentially causing "Thukk̄h́" to ourselves.**

For the book, "Human Secret", this section introduces a new term not previously used in the first book, *Read Before the meaning of your life is lesser* .

Let Uncle explain this term, which is commonly used in conversations across languages and religions.

# Secret 1st: The Secret of the Universe

The meaning of "Thukkh" will be thoroughly studied in this book until we find its true essence, allowing everyone to apply this knowledge and focus on **Creating Knowledge** about the root cause of their own "Thukkh".

Let's first understand the general meaning of Thukkh.

In Buddhism, Thukkh refers to an unbearable state of existence, a state of constraint which includes birth, aging, death, encountering what one dislikes, separation from what one loves, and unfulfilled desires.

For Westerners, especially English-speaking Christians, the term can be described with the following vocabulary:
- **Suffering**: Distress, physical discomfort, emotional unease, discontent, or pain.
- **Pain**: Physical discomfort.
- **Sorrow**: Sadness, heartache.
- **Grief**: Deep sadness, mourning.
- **Despair**: Hopelessness.
- **Agony**: Intense suffering or pain.
- **Torment**: Extreme pain or anguish.
- **Ailment**: Illness or disease.
- **Misfortune**: Bad luck or adversity.

# Secret 1st: The Secret of the Universe

**Note: The above information is derived from various online sources and does not represent my personal insights or writings.**

Returning to our primary content, if we somewhat perceive or feel the existence of the term "Thukkh",

At times, we "Thukkh" due to the words, actions, and thoughts of others affecting us. If we distinctly differentiate what's us from our environment, the path to truly discovering ourselves becomes simpler, and the "Thukkh" which arise unknowingly also diminish.

The study of humans in the dimension Uncle will guide us through is to let us see ourselves clearly.

The only one who'll constantly be there for us is, in reality, ourselves. Hence, *understanding ourselves is paramount in navigating our lives.*

For we've been constantly seeking others to care for us, neglecting self-care, leading to daily suffering from the absence of care.

# Secret 1st: The Secret of the Universe

If one doesn't understand this now, a day will come when one will, especially if one follows along.

However, if this isn't comprehensible,
let's ponder upon the following statement:

We are humans, Yet, unfamiliar with our kind. So, what should we truly comprehend?

Merely this thought might be enough to question, why even bother understanding humanity? If you genuinely see this, Let's embark on this journey together.

Uncle will share the tales and learnings about
 *"Humans" - a life subject about the "Ħạwkhid" and "ħạwcı"*

May we find joy in our voyage.
Uncle Mai Jaidi

*The two key terms "Ħạwkhid" and "ħạwcı" were central in the book "Read Before the meaning of your life is lesser." In this upcoming book, we will delve deeper into the workings of these two terms and their profound relationship with the secrets of humanity.*

# REFLECTIVE QUESTION:

# *IS THERE ANYONE WHO DOESN'T NEED TO UNDERSTAND ABOUT "HUMAN?"*

**AI Note for Chapter 1:**

Delving into the concept of "**Thuk̄k̇h**" or suffering, this chapter emphasizes the distinction between oneself and one's environment. By understanding this, one can effectively mitigate their own distress.

We revisit the significant terms "**H̄ạwkhid**" and "**h̄ạwcɪ**" from the previous volume, suggesting a profound exploration in future segments. Beyond the human perspective, a cosmic viewpoint emerges, offering a novel approach to our connection with the universe. This narrative challenges readers to rethink humanity's role in the broader scheme of existence, ending with a reflective query on our understanding of humanity.

## Note from the Author: *Secret 1*

*This chapter holds a pivotal essence: a novel cosmic perspective.* If we can truly perceive this at the "**Tạw rû̄s̥ụk**" level, it will influence our decisions. We would realize that we are a fragment of data, accountable for the data we intake and radiate. However, if we're not yet attuned to the "**Tạw rû̄s̥ụk**" depth, revisit this knowledge when making choices or decisions.

*Remark:* The term "Tạw rû̄s̥ụk" is the noun form of "rû̄s̥ụk or s̄ìng thì̂ rû̄s̥ụk." For a detailed understanding of this term, please refer to the book *"**Read Before the meaning of your life is lesser.**"*

*Your Note :* _____

_____

_____

_____

_____

_____

_____

*Your Note :* _____

_____

_____

_____

_____

_____

_____

_____

_____

_____

_____

_____

_____

_____

_____

_____

_____

_____

_____

"IF WE FEEL THE
IMPACT OF A PROBLEM,
IT INDICATES THAT WE
ARE A PART OF ITS
CAUSE."

Ekarach Chandon
Truth Quote 2005

Secret 2nd: Where's the Problem?

"HUMAN SECRET"

# Secret 2nd: Where's the Problem?

*From the first chapter we've studied,* we've come to realize that if our existence is called the universe, it comprises **two main parts: ourselves and our environment.** The existence of both us and our surroundings gives rise to **events and stories.** Without us, there wouldn't be any concern about the surroundings.

*Before embarking on this part of the journey,* Uncle wishes for you to listen to a tale, a story Uncle wants to share:

**Someone was struck by lightning and died.**

Imagine, for a moment, that it was us.

**We were struck by lightning and met our end.**
A problem arises with us:
**we were struck by lightning and perished.**

What was the cause of this issue?
Let's delve into this matter.

*A problem occurred:* We were struck dead by lightning...

# Secret 2nd: Where's the Problem?

*Whoever's given it thought,* let's delve deeper.
Whenever an event or a problem arises, as mentioned above, we quickly conclude that lightning is the problem.

We're struck dead by lightning.

On closer inspection, one will see that:
Us are the *"Human"*.

And what is the lightning that strikes?
It's the *"Surroundings"*.

So, who is the cause of the problem?
*"Human"* or the *"Surroundings"*?

Let's reconsider once more.

... *Zzzzzzz*...
Uncle's taking a quick nap and waiting. ...

For those who have read *"Read Before the Meaning of Your Life is Lesser"*... apply the perspective method from that book: *Rûṣu k -> khid -> rû̂*

# Secret 2nd: Where's the Problem?

*Lightning is caused by the environment.* Nowadays, most of us tend to think that: The environment is the source of problems.

If **Uncle** were to ask us again where the problem arises, We'd usually say it's the *lightning,* which is caused by the environment. ...

Or we might say, the problem lies with *"Humans".*

And what strikes them? *Lightning.* And where does lightning come from? The environment.

What should we refer to as *"lightning"* then?
**Uncle** distinguishes it as an *"event"* or *"phenomenon".*

These two terms, *"event"* and *"phenomenon",* are intricate. In future books, **Uncle** will delve deeper into differentiating these two terms.

**But when things happen quickly,** we tend to generalize and think: Humans are struck by lightning and that's a problem. Not clearly distinguishing where the problem really originates.

# Secret 2nd: Where's the Problem?

**Uncle observes:** Problems arise from people, while phenomena occur in the environment.

A lightning strike isn't a problem,
even if that lightning kills us.

**Now, Uncle would like us to consider and see clearly that:**
*Problems arise from "human",*
*Phenomena occur in the "environment".*

The issues we face come from both tangible phenomena that are evident, like a lightning strike, and abstract ones that are hard to discern, such as when someone we desire love from doesn't love us back.

**In the chapters we'll journey through together,**
Uncle will focus on a deeper understanding of the abstract problems we encounter.

At the very core of our being, delving from our "Directed to the Thinking Head" / *"Hạwkhid"* all the way to our "at the Heart" / *"hạw cı"*.

## Secret 2nd: Where's the Problem?

Right now, **Uncle** would like us to clearly understand that when problems arise, they stem from certain phenomena.

**If we don't want that problem to occur to us,** *then we shouldn't place ourselves in environments that lead to such events.*

What kind of environments are these?

**Reflect on it deeply.** Because the *"New Thought"* perspective that Uncle is presenting here suggests that the universe operates and relates in terms of *data structures* and *"data"*.

*"Those who fear getting struck by lightning and dying are not always those who have previously been struck by lightning."*

Please consider this before we continue our journey.
Stay safe, and don't get struck by lightning along the way.

Uncle Mai Jaidi

# AI Note on "Secret 2nd: Where's the Problem?"

- **Main Concept:** The chapter delves into understanding where problems arise, distinguishing between the self (*"Human"*) and the external factors (*"Surroundings"* or *"Environment"*).

- **Key Distinctions:**
    - a. **Human vs. Surroundings:** The universe of our existence comprises of ourselves (*"Human"*) and our environment (*"Surroundings"*). Events arise due to the interactions between these two.
    - b. **Event vs. Phenomenon:** The terms *"event"* and *"phenomenon"* are used interchangeably, but are intricate and will be further distinguished in future chapters. For now, an event such as a lightning strike is considered a phenomenon caused by the environment.

- **Narrative Device:** Uncle uses a simple yet impactful story of someone getting struck by lightning as an analogy. It's used to convey the idea that problems might not

*be purely due to external phenomena (like lightning), but rather our interaction with or presence within certain environments.*

## Note from the Author: *Secret 2* - A Thought to Ponder

The fear of death stemming from self-love has its benefits, ensuring we don't lead ourselves into problematic situations.

However, if our self-love and fear of death make us overly timid, how then can we journey forward? A life that remains stagnant and unprogressive is hardly distinguishable from a wasted existence.

Learning from history enlightens us on which paths are viable and what awaits at their ends. *It equips us with the courage to pursue the prosperity of our lives without excessive fear, and without carelessness that could lead us astray.*

*Your Note :* _____

_____

_____

_____

_____

_____

*Your Note :* _____

_____

_____

_____

_____

_____

_____

_____

_____

_____

_____

_____

_____

_____

_____

_____

_____

_____

_____

"WHEN WE
ACKNOWLEDGE THAT
WE ARE A CAUSE OF THE
PROBLEM, THE
RESOLUTION BEGINS."

Ekarach Chandon
Truth Quote 2005

Secret 3rd: The Best Solution Is?

"HUMAN SECRET"

..Maybe it's because we only learned how to solve other human's problems. We ourselves have never encountered our own problems...

# Secret 3rd: The Best Solution Is?

From the story of being struck by lightning, we realize that some problems, once they arise, we don't know how to solve. For instance, in a situation where we were hit by lightning and died, we might have to wait to solve it in our next life.

**So, what is the best way to address a problem?**
*Let's consider it together.*

Before diving into how to best solve a problem, let's ponder *why we fear lightning even though we've never been struck by it ourselves.*

It's because we don't want to make the same mistakes as those in the past, even though we've never experienced such an event. However, in the past, there were people who faced such issues, and they've compiled solutions.

This, Uncle calls **"learning"**.

# Secret 3rd: The Best Solution Is?

**Learning means rectifying the mistakes of the past, both of our own and others'.**

And rectifying mistakes isn't about hastily finding a way to get it right, But actually you have to find out. **"Why do we do it wrong?"**

It's not essential for every human to be struck by lightning to understand its fearsome nature. Once we recognize the external factors that might be dangerous to us, we steer clear. In doing so, problems are averted.

Uncle, not wanting to belabor the point, concludes: *The best solution to any problem is preventing it in the first place.* But be especially cautious, for some issues, once they arise, are irreparable in this lifetime—like being struck dead by lightning.

So, how do we learn to foresee and prevent these issues? The answer is simple: **Be diligent in learning.**

**Our lifespan is too short to learn everything firsthand. Thus, we must learn from the experiences of others.**

# Secret 3rd: The Best Solution Is?

Uncle once found the truth when reading literature as a child, especially the works of **Mark Twain**.

Reading a lot of ancient children's literature as a child leads to greater understanding "Human" as an adult.
Our mistakes then lessen.

When looking back at the best solutions, once we recognize that the problem arose from our involvement, we accept that the problem was due to us.

**Once we accept,**
**That is the beginning of the birth of "Payyā"**

When the prevention of problems takes place,
the best solutions emerge.

Start learning and accept when a problem arises with "Human", that "Human" is the cause of the problem.

*And the "Human" closest to start solving the problem is "Us".*

# Secret 3rd: The Best Solution Is?

Knowledge about **"Payyā"** in brief:

**"Payyā"** *is the state of seeing the world as it truly is. When we possess this state, the result is the capability to solve problems.*

If you wish to delve deeper into the topic of "Payyā", you can read in the book **Read Before the meaning of your life is lesser.** Information about "Payyā" starts on page 97, and chapter 11 in the said book provides more detailed insights.

For this book, let's initially define and get acquainted with this term. Future chapters will further our understanding of this word.

**Uncle has started solving, let's walk this path together. The problem of people that we will help solve together.**

Uncle Mai Jaidi

# AI Note on "Learning, Acceptance, and Payyā"

This discourse introduces us to a profound realization regarding problem-solving. **Beginning with the metaphor of being struck by lightning**—a problem we might not have a direct solution for in this life—it dives into the deeper nuances of understanding and confronting issues.

**Learning:** A primary emphasis is on the act of learning. Not just from personal experiences, but significantly from the experiences of others. **This idea is deeply rooted in understanding historical failures**, not to repeat them but to derive solutions from them.

As illustrated, **one doesn't need to experience the peril of lightning to understand its dangers;** learning from others provides the wisdom to prevent certain challenges.

**Acceptance:** Upon identifying a problem, recognizing our role or involvement in its inception is vital. It's about taking responsibility. Once we realize that the root cause of an issue is human involvement, **accepting it becomes the first step towards resolution.**

*This acceptance is not about blame but understanding.*

**Pạyyā:** This term, central to the narrative, is described as a **state of true comprehension of the world.** With Pạyyā, one gains the ability to address challenges effectively.

It's an enlightened state where the world is seen for what it truly is, enabling the possessor to **derive solutions based on reality.**

**In essence,** this piece is a call to action. To learn proactively, accept responsibly, and strive for the state of Pạyyā, for in these three concepts lies the secret to effective problem-solving.

**Note from the Author:** *Secret 3rd: The Best Solution Is?*
   **"Pạyyā comes from "US" who accepts wrongdoing."**

*Your Note :* _____

_____

_____

_____

_____

_____

*Your Note :* _____

_____

_____

_____

_____

_____

_____

_____

_____

_____

_____

_____

_____

_____

_____

_____

_____

_____

# "LEARNING, WHEN KNOWN, IS KNOWN BY ONESELF, NOT BY OTHERS."

Ekarach Chandon
Truth Quote 2005

Secret 4th: Who or What Surpasses Today's Scholarly Boundaries?

"HUMAN SECRET"

"...Sometimes, the problems we fail to see might be because we are blinded to them..."

## Secret 4th: Who or What Surpasses Today's Scholarly Boundaries?

Given the brevity of our lives, we can't possibly learn everything on our own. So, from whom should we learn about life?

**Who possesses the clearest and most profound understanding of "Human"?**

Tracing back centuries, even over two thousand years ago, we predominantly find the Buddha. Let's ponder upon what He discovered; *was it significant?*

He realized that there were underlying factors within us, influencing our perceptions and reactions. Depending on the mix of these factors - **greed/Lopha, anger/thoṡa, and delusion/moha** - it's akin to blending the three primary colors we learned to mix as children when painting.

**An excessive blend results in a dark, murky shade, while a minimal mix produces a light, clear white.**

# Secret 4th: Who or What Surpasses Today's Scholarly Boundaries?

What's fascinating is how He came to this knowledge. *For those curious about the depths of His realization, especially concerning the intricacies of human tendencies*, even more complex than discerning colors, further study is recommended.

It is **difficult** to know that the colors we see are the result of mixing three primary colors. As for what we can't see and how to perceive it, we won't discuss that here.

Just getting to truly know **greed, anger**, and **delusion** is difficult in itself.

But to understand ourselves, I, *Uncle*, rely on the framework of thought left by the wise. However, we'll stick to what we can relate to - our own "**S̄ing thī rū̄s̄ụk**".

The subject we're about to learn concerning humans is derived from A prophet who is skilled in knowledge about "**human**".

It should be enough for us to trust and follow.

Personally, Uncle holds a belief:

# Secret 4th: Who or What Surpasses Today's Scholarly Boundaries?

"Following the Buddha's path is never a foolish choice." ....
Why did Uncle say this?

Because the Buddha taught us not to believe anyone.
Don't believe even the Lord Buddha said it himself. Even
what he teaches us, the Lord Buddha still doesn't let us
believe.

The Buddha wants us to scrutinize until we truly see and
genuinely feel for ourselves. How then could we claim
superiority over scholars?

In an education system where we rely on scholars for
knowledge, Every time we reference an idea or knowledge,
we must attribute it to which scholar said it.

But with Lord Buddha's teachings, there's no such need.
When you know, you just know. It's something you realize
on your own.

The path one walks on, one's own life — if we don't
occasionally find our way by ourselves, how will we manage
not to get lost the day we have to walk alone?

## Secret 4th: Who or What Surpasses Today's Scholarly Boundaries?

**Let's just say that when it comes to Human subjects, we adopt methods akin to those taught by Lord Buddha.**
One can discern truths on their own. What Uncle is about to share stems from a learning journey that set benchmarks for self-evaluation. When assessing yourself, consider these benchmarks. If they strike a chord, delve deeper into self-reflection.

"*Do not hastily judge others.*
Dharma serves to help one understand oneself, rather than merely understanding the Dharma."

This knowledge, *Uncle gained it from creating knowledge of a student taught by Uncle.*

*When you know, you know. You can know for yourself.*

**Intriguingly,** over the past 2,500 years, billions have walked this earth. Many scholars have emerged.

Yet, only a handful have truly understood the essence of Dharma as taught by Lord Buddha, emphasizing the importance of personal realization over mere knowledge.

# Secret 4th: Who or What Surpasses Today's Scholarly Boundaries?

The significance lies in Lord Buddha's emphatic teaching: *Refrain from blind faith in his doctrines.* If you haven't truly grasped it, you can't genuinely "rûṣụk" it."

The fact that so many people have studied the Dharma for so long without achieving enlightenment is a testament to the importance of self-realization.

**It is only by understanding ourselves that we can truly understand the Dharma.**

*This is why the Lord Buddha emphasized so strongly:*
*Do not blindly believe his teachings.*
*If you really don't know, you can't "rûṣụk" it yourself.*

**Don't follow him. I don't know who to follow.**

Uncle must take his leave now. Hurry up and follow along. Wishing all of us good fortune.

It's a memory.

Uncle Mai Jaidi

**AI Note on "Secret 4th: Who or What Surpasses Today's Scholarly Boundaries?**

*Chapter 4* embarks on a journey to unravel a deeper understanding of human nature, with its foundations deeply rooted in Buddha's teachings. Uncle uses a *vivid* analogy, likening human tendencies such as **greed, anger,** and **delusion** to the blending of primary colors, highlighting the complex tapestry of human emotions.

Rather than viewing Buddha's teachings merely as doctrines, Uncle underscores them as invaluable tools for introspection and personal realization.

The chapter emphasizes the need for individuals to prioritize personal understanding over blind faith, highlighting the significance of self-awareness and **introspection.** This core message, drawn from Buddha's teachings, propels Uncle to champion introspection and urges readers to challenge and introspect their beliefs.

The overarching essence of the chapter centers on the pivotal role of **self-understanding** as the key to decoding broader truths about life.

"HUMAN SECRET 4TH" WHO OR WHAT SURPASSES TODAY'S SCHOLARLY BOUNDARIES?

52

## Key Quotes:

- *"He realized that there were underlying factors within us, influencing our perceptions and reactions."*
- *"Just getting to truly know greed, anger, and delusion is difficult in itself."*
- **"The Buddha wants us to scrutinize until we truly see and genuinely feel for ourselves."**
- "Do not hastily judge others. Dharma serves to help one understand oneself, rather than merely understanding the Dharma."

## Note from the Author: *Secret 4th"*
### *Who or What Surpasses Today's Scholarly Boundaries?*

*"How do we know if we're not straying off the path?*

*And if we never care about where the journey will take us, we will never truly know if we have lost our way."*

*Your Note :* _____

_____

_____

_____

_____

*Your Note :* _____

_____

_____

_____

_____

_____

_____

_____

_____

_____

_____

_____

_____

_____

_____

# STARTING POINT FOR SELF-DEVELOPMENT:

## "DON'T LIE TO YOURSELF AND DENY WHAT IS YOUR "FEELINGS"."

Ekarach Chandon
Truth Quote 2005

Secret 5th: What Drives Us to Think?

"HUMAN SECRET"

## Secret 5th: What Drives Us to Think?

**What triggers our thoughts?**
What do we see when we look within?

Some try to convey that suffering arises from our "Kileš".
But how? We seem blind to it. It's unclear what they mean
by "Kileš". So, what do we actually perceive in such
moments?

**Where is this "Kileš" located?** It governs us, so they say,
but we fail to see it. How should we then proceed?
Uncle then wonders, *what are we observing?*
*What do we actually discern?*

Most of what Uncle will discuss next revolves around
abstract problems, issues that deal more with our inner
world than merely our physical form.

We won't be discussing lightning strikes anymore but rather
the issues that remain unseen, those intangible occurrences.
**Let's delve into matters of the mind...**

# Secret 5th: What Drives Us to Think?

When events impact us, especially those causing harm, like when someone does good or bad to us, what happens within? Where does this mischief lie? We should find and observe this "Kileś" that controls us.

If you find this part hard to grasp, Uncle suggests reading another book titled *"Read Before the meaning of your life is lesser,"* particularly chapters 3, 4, and 5. Let's continue.

Whenever something affects us, no matter which sense is involved, The "sense" here refers to the ear, eye, nose, tongue, body, and mind - six in total.

The mind does truly exist.

Science might say it doesn't, but what Uncle is teaching us isn't based on current science that uses tools for measurements nor is it a religious method that believes without knowing what it believes in.

But Uncle speaks of what we can truly perceive; do these things really exist? This is a subject about our *Ḥạwkhid/ thoughts* and *hạwcı/heart* as previously mentioned.

# Secret 5th: What Drives Us to Think?

**Let's delve into the concept of the 'heart'.** Do humans truly understand the existence of the heart?

There are age-old phrases that hint at its presence.
Terms such as *joyful heart*, *heartache*, and *heartbreak* suggest it might exist.

These phrases were crafted by our ancestors, but it's crucial not to be easily convinced. A good disciple of Buddha shouldn't believe everything, even the words of the Buddha himself, as written and spoken by him.

When we **overthink**, the stress is felt in the head. This stress is a result of excessive thinking. However, this is different from when we feel deep emotions, such as heartbreak or joy. These feelings seem to emanate from the chest area.

It's fascinating how certain impacts make us *feel instantly*, even before our thoughts catch up. I refer to this as **"S̄ing thī̀ rū̄s̄ụk"**, distinct from "emotion" or "feeling".

By nature, while our brain has a vast neural system,
But the heart doesn't have such a large nervous system.

# Secret 5th: What Drives Us to Think?

Yet, when emotional impacts occur, nature leads us to feel them in our chest, where the heart resides. This indicates to us its existence. **We humans have a heart** and cannot deny its presence.

So, what is the abstract concept of the heart that nature wants us to comprehend? Let's explore this together.

Lastly, let me revisit the distinction between '**S̄ing thī̀ rûs̄ụk**' and 'emotion' or 'feeling' once more.

**S̄ing thī̀ rûs̄ụk** arise before our thoughts can grasp them. Emotions or feeling are seen, and the thoughts causing them can be caught.

The duration of '**S̄ing thī̀ rûs̄ụk**' varies: some are short-lived, others long. We can't define them in measurable time units, it depends on our self-awareness.

*As Uncle* mentions, observing our thoughts frequently can make us more attuned to our '**S̄ing thī̀ rûs̄ụk**', allowing us to recognize them faster.

# Secret 5th: What Drives Us to Think?

For beginners, the phases of 'S̄ìng thǐ rûs̄ụk' might be elusive because they can't locate the starting point of their thoughts. This awareness comes with practice and self-realization. *The observation points that Uncle suggests are vital.*

**Therefore, when something affects us, the sequence goes as follows:**

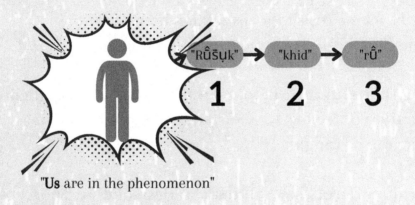

"**Us** are in the phenomenon"

*Picture 2. The processes that happen within us*

*In the initial stage, we will "Rûs̄ụk" (feel it). In the next stage, we will "khid" (think about it). And finally, we will "rû" (know it).*

Uncle would like to bring up an old example from the book *"Read Before the Meaning of Your Life is Lesser"* for us to revisit.

# Secret 5th: What Drives Us to Think?

**Example:**

*We will feel that something is hitting us. Uncle thinks that uncle gave this example. We should have knowledge that is detailed enough to recognize that What's affecting us?*

*This one uses the body around the face as a receiver.*
*After receiving it, you "Rûṣụk" ( will feel) "khid" (think) and "rû" (know that), we realized that hey, I got punched.*

*After this, uncle still didn't explain. What happened to us next?*

That's a simple example for us to read and easily understand what feeling, thinking, and knowing are like.

**Here's another example:**

*Imagine when we use mercury to measure temperature. The expansion of mercury signifies a change, but we don't exactly know what kind of change. We have to compare it, set a standard, and deduce that if it expands to a certain level, it will read a certain temperature. In general, the standards for mercury have already been set for us, so we just know without really understanding the reasoning behind it.*

# Secret 5th: What Drives Us to Think?

This example is to make us understand that our abstract nature also has scientific processes that can be explained to understand its mechanisms.

For deeper topics about these scientific mechanisms, Uncle will write in a separate book specifically dedicated to it.

Now, we understand that what we need to perceive is 'S̄ìng thī̀ rûs̄ụk'. '**S̄ìng thī̀ rûs̄ụk**' is intricate enough that we can recognize it without going as deep as the '**Cit**'/psyche.

The latter is elusive, and we often can't pinpoint its exact location - *whether it's subconscious or above the conscious. We often can't find it.* What Uncle wants us to do is to observe ourselves, to find out how we '**Rûs̄ụk**'.

*This* '**S̄ìng thī̀ rûs̄ụk**' *is what connects us to our inner* '**Kiles̄**'.

**Uncle's Note:** For those who find themselves puzzled at this juncture, wondering about the nature of '*Rûs̄ụk*', '*khid*', and '*rū̂*', and *specifically, what exactly* '*S̄ìng thī̀ rûs̄ụk*' *is*, you may revisit the book **"Read Before the meaning of your life is lesser,"** specifically **Chapters 3, 4, and 5**, as *previously mentioned by me.*

# Secret 5th: What Drives Us to Think?

*Uncle earnestly implores you to grasp tse concepts. Familiarizing yourself with them will prove immensely valuable in this lifetime.* **Understanding yourself is truly worth the investment.**

**Just this may not be enough** for us to properly train ourselves. If Uncle could suggest a method that *Uncle's used* effectively, it's this: *Every time you feel something, respond to it before you think or act.* Ask yourself, **why did I do that?** This is the main principle in recognizing your own feelings.

In the beginning, you might not catch it right away. Why did I feel that way? **Why did I think, speak, or act like that?** Regularly practice every time you breathe. You'll start to notice your own imperfections.

Another technique Uncle uses and recommends, especially for those who work with him, is this: ***Buy an Digital Recorder*** with a recording feature. Record your conversations with others. Listen to them later and ask yourself, **why did I say that? What was I feeling when I said that?**

This is especially effective for those who often engage in conversations with others.

# Secret 5th: What Drives Us to Think?

If your job involves meetings and consultations,
**record the sessions.** You'll definitely see results.

Listen and continuously question your statements.
*Ask yourself, 'Why did I say that? What's the purpose behind it?'*

You'll start seeing your feelings more clearly, quickly,
and in detail. This is a practical technique.

Once you recognize your feelings,
further reflection will make it clear:
What are the predominant imperfections driving us?
*This training phase helps you quickly recognize these imperfections.*

It's the beginning of addressing life's issues.
Recognize and accept your imperfections.

If you reach the level Uncle has trained at, you're already
remarkable in understanding your imperfections.

You don't need to delve deep into your 'Cit'/psyche right
away. **Start by simply understanding your 'S̄ìng thī̀ rū̂sụ̄k'.**

# Secret 5th: What Drives Us to Think?

What we 'rûs̄u̠k' is the gateway to our true self. Embracing our 's̄ìng thī rûs̄u̠k' is the ladder to becoming the best version of ourselves.

The term "being aware" or "feeling conscious" is something we often hear.

- 's̄ìng thī rûs̄u̠k' the sounds that touch our ears.

- 's̄ìng thī rûs̄u̠k' the light that touches our eyes.

- 's̄ìng thī rûs̄u̠k' the scents that touch our nose.

- 's̄ìng thī rûs̄u̠k' the flavors that touch our tongue.

- 's̄ìng thī rûs̄u̠k' the forces that touch our body.

- *So*, what touches the heart for it to feel?

Signing off,

Uncle Mai Jaidi

# AI Note on "Secret 5th: What Drives Us to Think?

**Exploring self-observation, the importance of feelings and thoughts, and the connection between the heart and brain in the human perception pathway.**

- Self-observation and the importance of introspection to understand one's feelings.
- Emotions and sensations that arise before thinking, and the difficulty in locating and understanding the 'Cit' or 'psyche'.
- The connection between the heart and the brain, and feelings that originate from the chest area when emotionally impacted.
- The process of perception when an event occurs: feel -> think -> then realize.
- Methods of learning and practice to understand oneself.

*Do you want to know where our 'thoughts' and 'feelings' come from? Secret 5 will take you on a journey to explore the connection between the heart and the brain and how to observe your own feelings and thoughts to better understand yourself. Don't miss out!*

The key quote of the secret is:

**What we "rûṣ̣uk" is the gateway to our true self.**

This quote emphasizes the importance of understanding and embracing our feelings in order to understand ourselves better. The passage explains that our feelings, or "s̄ìng thî rûṣ̣uk", are the first thing that we experience when we are affected by something. Before we can think about or analyze the situation, we feel it. These feelings are connected to our inner "kiles̄", or imperfections.

By understanding and embracing our feelings, we can begin to identify and address the imperfections that are driving us. This is the beginning of the journey to becoming the best version of ourselves.

The passage also provides two practical tips for developing our awareness of our feelings:

- Every time you feel something, respond to it before you think or act. Ask yourself, why did I do that?

- Record your conversations with others and listen to them later. Ask yourself, why did I say that? What was I feeling when I said that?

By regularly practicing these tips, we can develop a deeper understanding of ourselves and our true selves.

**Note from the Author:** *Secret 5th: What Drives Us to Think?*

## Thought Unlock Secrets

*"How to measure something that is sizeless using a measuring tool that has a size?"*

*Your Note :* _____

_____

_____

_____

_____

_____

_____

_____

_____

_____

*Your Note :* _____

_____

_____

_____

_____

_____

_____

_____

_____

_____

_____

_____

_____

_____

_____

_____

_____

_____

"AS SOON AS WE FEEL
THAT SOMETHING IS NOT
ENOUGH, WE SEE OUR
'KILEŠ', WHICH IS NEVER
ENOUGH."

Ekarach Chandon
Truth Quote 2005

Secret 6th: When Will It Be Enough?

"HUMAN SECRET"

"If you can't see your heart,
how can you know when it's enough?"

# Secret 6th: When Will It Be Enough?

Let's explore how **"Tạw rū̄s̄uk"** relate to "kileš" .
Uncle (In this book series, I will refer to myself as 'Uncle.)
wants to highlight a point of transformation that everyone
should consider. *What transformation, you ask?* As you delve
deeper into the next few chapters, you'll realize that just
like water has states – solid, liquid, and gas – **humans too
have their internal transitions.**

**State of Being** Soon, we will discover what state we are in.
For now, let's focus on the concept of sufficiency.

Imagine this scenario: You possess something you truly
cherish, be it food, toys, money, or even power (especially
for the adults reading). And you refuse to share it with
anyone.

*Uncle often contemplates using food as an analogy because it's
simple and relatable.* Some may resonate with other objects,
but the essence remains: how do we feel deep inside when
we're unwilling to share?

# Secret 6th: When Will It Be Enough?

When we indulge in our favourite dish and don't offer it to anyone, **what emotions stir within?** *Dive deep, venture further into your 'ŝìng thî rûŝụk', and constantly question why.*

It's not just about the delight of taste that stops us from sharing. There's a profound sentiment underneath.

Before reading further, ponder upon your deepest feelings when it comes to your favourite food.

Articulate your emotions or feelings in words (or linguistic symbols) that aptly express your 'ŝìng thî rûŝụk'. If food doesn't resonate with you, perhaps you're the type who shares food all the time, then switch to another analogy. Uncle uses food because often, when we think back to our childhood, the most tangible objects of desire were treats. When in our mother's womb, *aside from the elements that made us, the first thing we receive from others is nourishment.*

If you've never experienced withholding food from someone, try to recall your younger days until the memory surfaces. If it still eludes, shift the focus, and contemplate as Uncle suggests.

# Secret 6th: When Will It Be Enough?

Let's consider what Uncle believes as to why we don't share with others. Uncle sees there are three main reasons:

1. **Ignorance** - Not realizing that others also need to eat, to have, and to use.
2. **Fear** - Fearing that what we eat, what we have, and what we use will not be sufficient.
3. **Desire for Everything** - Wanting to eat, to have, and to use as much as possible for oneself.

These three characteristics reveal why, at times, we might refrain from sharing. When we're unable to share, it's often because we're influenced by one of these three states. **Recognizing these '*Rûṣu k*' unveils the underlying '*kileṣ*' that often control us:**

- *The first characteristic represents **ignorance** lacking due to unawareness.* '**Mo̅ha**'
- *The second embodies **fear**: lacking because of the fear of insufficiency.* '**Loṗha**'
- *The third, the **desire for everything**, showcases an unwillingness to lose out, a lack stemming from wanting the most.* '**Thoṣa**'

# Secret 6th: When Will It Be Enough?

*Understanding these 'kileš' helps us reflect on our 'S̄ìng thī̀ rū̂s̄ụk'.* By recognizing which 'kileš' dominates us at any given moment, **"What are our main 'kileš' that use us? Accept yourself, then start using your 'kileš'."**

Initially, reflect on these **'S̄ìng thī̀ rū̂s̄ụk'** and discern which 'kileš' is secretly influencing you.

Revisiting the concept of sufficiency, many discussions circle around it. Sufficiency primarily relates to the heart. *When one feels generous enough to share with others, that is sufficiency.*

The capacity to share varies among individuals. It's like clothing sizes. Not everyone can wear the same small size. Before advising someone to opt for a smaller size, it's essential to help them recognize their actual size. Educate them on the repercussions of being overweight—more illnesses and a lack of energy—and the disadvantages of being underweight. Then, guide them to care for their health optimally. Yet, before anything, once they recognize their size, teach them to choose clothing that fits.

*True sufficiency arises when the heart understands this essence.*

# Secret 6th: When Will It Be Enough?

"One must train the mind to see 'pạyyạā', to avoid being manipulated by 'kileš'. When blinded by 'kileš', the heart may act unknowingly, possibly causing harm or dividing others. But if we employ 'pạyyạā', we not only avoid harm but are also in a better position to support others.

*In many more books to come, I, 'Uncle', will convey deeper insights to guide us in our actions, enabling transformative change to a better self – the version of ourselves we consciously choose. A version that effortlessly finds joy.*

*We shouldn't suffer unnecessarily when we know how to harness our inner wisdom. Let's leave it at this for now, reflecting upon an old Buddhist proverb that says, 'No one can make every grain of sand identical in size, just as no one can make every person the same.' We, humans, are inherently diverse, and thankfully, we aren't grains of sand. We have the choice to shape ourselves as we feel fit.*

**"Every human being can become noble through training."**

Otherwise, these words might prove insufficient.
Wishing everyone happiness, Uncle Mai Jaidi

## AI Note on "Secret 6th: When Will It Be Enough?

Reflects the author's thoughts and beliefs about emotions, intelligence, and the essence of being human. The author poses questions about intelligence and feelings, emphasizing the importance of aligning one's actions with personal beliefs. The content presents ideas that could aid in fostering happiness in life and self-development.

**Notable Truth Quote:** From the translated content, a quote that speaks to the truth about human nature and society is:

*"No one can make every grain of sand the same size; just as no one can make every person identical."*

This highlights the inherent diversity and individuality of humans. Yet, in society, we have the choice to recognize and embrace these differences, which can foster happiness and harmony in the community.

**Note from the Author:**
**Secret 6th: When Will It Be Enough?**

"Every human being can become noble through training."

"What kind of training can lead to such nobility?"

*Your Note :* _____

_____

_____

_____

_____

_____

_____

_____

_____

_____

_____

_____

_____

_____

_____

_____

_____

# "LEARNING ARISES FROM CORRECTING PAST MISTAKES, BUT PẠ̄ỴỴĀ COMES FROM TAKING RESPONSIBILITY."

Ekarach Chandon
Truth Quote 2005

Secret 7th: Why So Much Suffering?

"HUMAN SECRET"

"Thukīkh́" creates problems,
"Pạyyā" creates happiness.

# Secret 7th: Why So Much Suffering?

The Secret Uncle would like to introduce involves a unique Thai term, pivotal to understanding oneself. That term is "Thukīkh́". Even within the Thai language itself, it's hard to find someone who can truly define this term. From what Uncle could gather, here's what you should know:

The term "Thukīkh́" in Thai has its roots from Buddhism, which is widely accepted in Thai culture, especially in Buddhist teachings about the **"Four Noble Truths"**. One of those truths speaks extensively of "Thukīkh́". It is evident that the term "Thukīkh́" carries profound and multifaceted meanings depending on the context. It doesn't solely refer to physical pain, but encompasses emotional distress, loss, imperfections in life, and sorrow.

*"Thukīkh́" is pain, sorrow, and loss, both physically and mentally.*

The meaning of "Thukīkh́" may vary depending on the context, but generally, it signifies pain experienced both physically and emotionally.

# Secret 7th: Why So Much Suffering?

**According to Buddhist principles:**

Suffering is one of the **Four Noble Truths** and holds significant meaning in the teachings of Lord Buddha. Under Buddhist doctrine, "suffering" describes the pain, imperfection, and the natural changes of life.

And among the crucial doctrines in Buddhism, one stands out as **"The Four Noble Truths."** In Buddhism, they are the principles that Lord Buddha emphasized as the truths that humans should understand. And "suffering" is a part of these truths that Lord Buddha taught about the reality of life.

Explaining "Thukkh" is challenging in English as there are various contexts and synonyms like *Suffering, Pain, Misery, Sorrow, Grief, Distress, Anguish, Hardship, Affliction,* and *Trouble.* It becomes extremely complex if not for the specific term used.

As for explaining "Thukkh" in the context Uncle wants us to understand and apply in our lives, it's not complicated. All we need to do is examine it in detail, based on the continuation from the previous secret.

# Secret 7th: Why So Much Suffering?

More knowledge about

The Four Noble Truths consist of:

1. Dukkha (Suffering): A state of discomfort, a situation that is hard to endure, a state of oppression, encountering what one does not love, separation from what one loves, and unsatisfied desires.
2. Samudaya (The Cause of Suffering): The main cause of suffering is "craving" or human desires and attachments.
3. Nirodha (The End of Suffering): The end of suffering is a state where humans can avoid or solve their problems, which can be achieved by following the Dharma (teachings).
4. Magga (The Path leading to the End of Suffering): This is the practice leading to Nirodha, or the cessation of suffering, teaching the right way of living to end suffering.

The Four Noble Truths are crucial in problem-solving. Uncle introduces these for those who want to study deeper. Why did Uncle choose to use this term?

# Secret 7th: Why So Much Suffering?

From our previous discussions, *it's evident how* **Kileś** *shape our* *Śìng thî rûśụk.* And what causes us the most "Thuk**k̄h**"? It's the feeling of wanting.

**The desire to have, the desire to be, the desire to own.**

Let's take these three desires for now. I, Uncle, am unsure if there are others. **When our desires are unmet, it leads to suffering. Consider this diagram.**

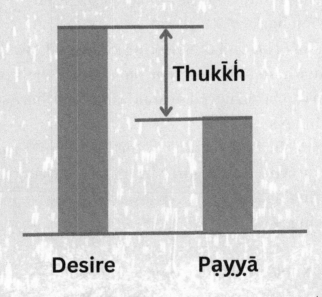

*Picture 3. Picture showing the cause of "Thukk̄h"*

# Secret 7th: Why So Much Suffering?

If we possess little 'pạyyā' but abundant desires, we experience immense 'Thukkh'. The magnitude of our 'Thukkh' depends on the disparity between our desires and 'pạyyā'. The greater the disparity, the deeper 'Thukkh'. To alleviate this 'Thukkh', one must either enhance their 'pạyyā' or diminish their desires.

Many dharmas teachings aim to ensure that our desires don't overshadow our inherent 'pạyyā'. They either focus on amplifying 'pạyyā' to match our desires or curtailing our desires to suit our 'pạyyā', ensuring peace.

If we can minimize our desires to a point where they virtually don't exist, and if our 'pạyyā' remains even slightly intact, then we won't 'Thukkh'.

When desires exceed our 'pạyyā', 'Thukkh' ensues. We feel the pain even before we can pinpoint the root of the problem.

At times, we remain oblivious to our true desires. What is the utmost desire in life? Without recognizing it, 'Thukkh' emerges, leading to unseen problems.

# Secret 7th: Why So Much Suffering?

If our 'pąyyā' is insufficient, we fail to identify the root of these issues. What do we truly desire in life? To solve these problems, we must extinguish these needs and desires.

**Whether by relinquishing these wants or by fulfilling them. But if we don't even know what to relinquish or what to seek, the path remains obscured.**

**I haven't discussed which method is superior;**
It all boils down to each individual's predilections.

Here, where the best method hasn't been debated, it's up to each person's curiosity.

*We won't discuss the notions of merits and sins here, as it's an often-discussed topic.*

"As for the matters of virtue and sin, their meanings according to the process that Uncle has derived from his knowledge creation are detailed in a separate book.

*Uncle will gradually write and share about this because it's a knowledge that Uncle categorizes under Meta-Physics."*

# Secret 7th: Why So Much Suffering?

Instead, let's **delve into the secrets of us, humans.**

Once we unravel these secrets, we'll be at a crossroad to decide which path to take. Uncle believes every human can think for themselves. All we need is a framework for contemplation. Talking about merits and sins in today's age, which can't be empirically proven, is a futile exercise.

The modern, sharp-witted youth will dismiss such discussions. Let's utilize our intellect to uncover the secrets of mankind on our own. If someone sees merit or sin, let them perceive it individually. Uncle feels it's far better than being told what to see.

Currently, **if desires surpass 'payya',** we 'Thuk̄kh'.

To alleviate 'Thuk̄kh', we can either enhance our 'payya' or suppress our desires. **'Payya' isn't mere intelligence; it's the ability to perceive the world as it truly is.**

When we see the truth, problem-solving becomes straightforward. If our perception is flawed, then solutions become elusive.

# Secret 7th: Why So Much Suffering?

It's akin to attempting to **untangle a knotted rope**. If we're unaware of the knot's intricacies and still try to untie it, our ignorance only tightens the tangle.

*"The Cause of 'pạyyā'"*, **Uncle** often emphasizes, **is the sense of responsibility for the future of...**

Whatever the thing, that's how big the 'pạyyā' is.

It's strange, for instance, if it's just about us alone, the desire can be both high and low. But when the responsibility for the future of something grows, our inherent desire in the matter diminishes. The 'Thukkh' we experience is of a different kind.

It's a 'Thukkh' to know what 'Thukkh' is, what we desire, and where the doubts in our hearts lie.

Thus, with more 'pạyyā', our desires reduce on their own, and happiness becomes easier.

*Uncle once said, 'Thukkh' indeed causes problems, but 'pạyyā' brings happiness.*

# Secret 7th: Why So Much Suffering?

Understanding the dharma of Lord Buddha is profoundly challenging.

Without ever seeing the heart and its feelings, mere thinking might not be sufficient for comprehension.

Let us steadfastly observe our hearts, recognizing what we desire most. The day we encounter the highest desire in life, we'll realize that we were born in this life to resolve the doubts about this very desire.

**Wishing everyone happiness.** Remember well: *'payyā'*, *'payyā'*, *'payyā'*. Farewell, and good luck.

Uncle Mai Jaidi

## AI Note: Exploring Intelligence and Desires

- Desires and their relationship with intelligence: When our desires are intangible and not based on possessions or materiality, intelligence allows us to see reason and feel contentment.
- "Uncle" advises introspection: Understanding and recognizing our own desires and feelings is an essential step towards happiness and comprehending the Dharma teachings of Lord Buddha.
- Understanding intelligence in a spiritual context: While suffering presents challenges, intelligence offers contentment. Possessing intelligence can make us feel content and fulfilled in our life.
- Realizing true happiness: When we encounter the utmost desires in our life, contentment and happiness are realized as we understand and address these desires.

**Note from the Author:**
**Secret 7th: Why So Much Suffering?**

**"Little Life Insights from the 'Perils of Offspring' "**

I, Uncle, too indulge in gaming. However, I'm selective about the games I play, and I always advise my loved ones to recognize that with games, it's all about **choice**.

*Now, how to make these choices? Let me guide you on this.*

Have you ever pondered if playing games, especially those where you simply drag the mouse towards a monster, and voilà, it dies; you earn items and experience, becomes truly worth your time? Such games fuel your urge for more - more items, more character abilities, more experiences.

The more experience you gain, the more curious you become about the potential upgradations. But, is the sole skill of dragging the mouse repeatedly truly enriching for your life?

Think about it. Hours spent, eyes glued to the screen, with increasing desires and abilities limited to just moving a mouse. Now, picture a young child growing up, learning mainly from such games.

Can you imagine the potential troubles and challenges in their life stemming from these limited skills?
The continuous longing to achieve more, not realizing the scale of real-life challenges that await.

Take a look at the Picture 3. Picture showing the cause of "Thukkh" to gain a better perspective.

*Your Note :* _____

_____

_____

_____

_____

_____

_____

_____

_____

_____

_____

_____

_____

_____

_____

_____

_____

_____

# "FREEDOM: WHERE IS IT LOCATED? ONLY OUR HEARTS TRULY KNOW."

Ekarach Chandon
Truth Quote 2005

Secret 8th: Which Path
Leads to **True Freedom**?

"HUMAN SECRET"

"...No matter how far you travel, if you don't reach your own heart, you won't find freedom..."

# Secret 8th: Which Path Leads to True Freedom?

Desire: One thing humans continually yearn for is the desire to be free from desires.
This is quite profound. Intelligence needs to be elevated and desires minimized.

How can we reach this point when we live in the present?
We need to eat, work needs to be done. If one becomes a hermit, Uncle says go for it.

True freedom like that is attainable. Rise up, reject society,
Embark on a journey in search of freedom. Perhaps,
Embarking on a quest for life's meaning would be wise,
If we don't question anything in our current way of life.

For the young ones, how can they do such a thing?
The burden of parents' feelings hasn't been released yet.

Some, even in their old age, have never alleviated their parents' concerns if they can stand on their own.

# Secret 8th: Which Path Leads to True Freedom?

Seeking freedom would make their parents' hearts break.

By the time they *enter the workforce and bear responsibilities,* achieving such a goal becomes increasingly difficult.

And if, once everything is done, we have to return to our usual lives, Searching for money, for sustenance, for spending, in our current ways of life.

*Is the freedom we experienced then, true freedom, or just a figment of our imagination?*

If after the journey, our lives are still governed by the significance of money to our souls, Then perhaps, *the freedom we thought we had, wasn't real – it was just a thought.*

How can we always feel free?

*"Uncle" believes that we should seek the true meaning of freedom,*

One that's feasible and resonates with our current lives. Shouldn't we explore a new perspective together?

# Secret 8th: Which Path Leads to True Freedom?

Once we've found answers to our questions in life,
*who would want to try living the life of a hermit or a seeker?*
A life not bound by the capitalist world?
That's up to each individual's decision.

Right now, *Uncle* is trying to find a perspective that allows us to experience *freedom*, even while existing in the *capitalist world*. Simply put, the capitalist world is a world where we exchange money for the necessities of life and many other desires.

*Freedom means having sovereignty and being one's own master.*

*Uncle has been contemplating the perspectives we hold regarding* **freedom** *in relation to ourselves.*
We must discern what constitutes our being.

On a level that's easy to see, not complex or too profound, we consist of:

- The body - This is understood as our physical form.
- The thought - This refers to the thoughts that arise in our head, and

# Secret 8th: Which Path Leads to True Freedom?

- The spirit - This may seem elusive, not knowing exactly where it is, but to say it's nonexistent would be false. For when we delve deeply into self-study, it's unclear what drives us to think. Uncle calls this deeper, more subtle element the spirit, though it's hard to explain. It's up to us to perceive when we feel something more delicate than our thoughts, and that which becomes our identity - we may call it spirit.

The journey to true freedom from the spirit is not considered here; let's just focus on the first two stages,Because even uncle myself did not reach that point within this book.

**Stage 1: Freedom from the body** - This is seen from an angle to benefit life without becoming a slave to our own body.

**First Perspective:** There are no restrictions caused by the body, like when reading a book, but the body is heavy, lazy, becoming a hindrance; this arises from the lazy body.

**We become a slave, with the body as an obstacle in doing anything.**

## Secret 8th: Which Path Leads to True Freedom?

**Second Perspective:** Desires that the body demands make us slaves to it. For instance, when faced with delicious food, we eat non-stop, unable to control ourselves. Encountering pleasing sensations, we become engrossed even though we know we shouldn't; we can't restrain the desires arising from our body's sensations. Uncle calls this also a lack of freedom from the body.

Where there is no freedom from the body, there is much **Thuk̄kh́**.

**Third Perspective:** When the body deteriorates, **Thuk̄kh́** arises. We seek ways to prevent deterioration, to pull and adorn, until we no longer know where happiness lies. **Thuk̄kh́** because of a deteriorating body is also a form of bondage. *We care for our bodies, but it shouldn't dominate our entire life.* Some people, if we observe the lack of freedom from the body **from this third perspective**, will realize that it actually occurs because our thoughts control us; we are slaves to our thoughts.

This is the result that begins to make us see that we are not free from our thoughts.

# Secret 8th: Which Path Leads to True Freedom?

*The freedom of thought we shall consider has angles for the benefit of contemporary life as follows:*

**Step 2: Freedom from thoughts.** Many people attempt to explain that our differing thoughts are independent, while the very differences we think are, in fact, **employing us.** The freedom from thought that Uncle will guide us to *contemplate is the emancipation from being slaves to our thoughts.*

A perspective that allows thoughts to not hinder any action, this is for the benefit of engaging in what we desire. Have you noticed when we want to do something, we consider it good and proper, but we hesitate due to fear of others' disapproval because it deviates from societal norms? Uncle calls this not yet being free in thought. What enslaves us is our knowledge, the framework of our lack of freedom from thought. By considering what we **rûṣụk**, we understand why we have such thoughts. Observing our **S̄ing thȉ rûṣụk** paves the way to freedom from our thoughts, preventing them from being obstacles in life henceforth. **Uncle refers to this as true intellectual freedom.**

Let's consider this one aspect of thought, leaving a little more to ponder:

# Secret 8th: Which Path Leads to True Freedom?

**When thinking of doing versus not doing, the dedication differs. These are the little nuggets of life.**

As we consider why we think the way we do because of what we **rûṣụk**, we begin a journey to perceive things finer than our thoughts. For Uncle, **this thought is still coarse** because what we see and **rûṣụk** exists within our head.

The finer things, those we cannot grasp or catch with thought, are the beginnings of subtlety. The spirit is delicate at that level. Train to observe our thoughts, to look at the knowledge enveloping us until it's clear.

*Then we can use thoughts without being used by them, achieving true freedom from thought.*

Let us think and consider as Uncle has written in the introduction. Uncle wrote this because he believes every human can think for themselves.

What Uncle conveys is not to dictate what we should or should not do, but rather to offer another perspective for us to contemplate, to discern our life paths for ourselves.

# Secret 8th: Which Path Leads to True Freedom?

What we must consider in thinking is to diligently discern why we think that way. There are two foundations for thinking:

1. Thinking derived from the knowledge we have received.
2. Thinking arising from the **Sīng thī rūsụk** we experience within ourselves.

Let us examine more clearly because every time we think, influences from both bases mix in every time. When we see the cause that enters into our thinking every time, we then have the freedom to think.

**Thoughts will become our tool.** We no longer have to fall under the influence of our own thoughts.

Persistently consider every time, every story, every event that the environment impacts us. When we see our own thoughts, we then examine why we think that way.

**The freedom that arises is felt by our own heart; there's no need to travel.** The practice towards true freedom occurs within our own mind.

## Secret 8th: Which Path Leads to True Freedom?

When we have no doubts in the current capitalist path, we can embark on the journey towards a higher freedom, the freedom of the spirit.

Joy in the journey towards freedom to all,
Uncle Mai

## Revisiting the Essence of Freedom:

**Bodily Freedom:** Not to be enslaved by one's own physical form, overcoming obstacles that arise from bodily demands.

**Thought freedom:** Not to be a thrall to one's own thoughts, surmounting barriers born of the mind.

**Spiritual Freedom:** The stage leading to a higher moral state beyond that of an ordinary person,

The last point I'd like to leave aside for now.
Uncle hasn't mentioned it yet in this book.

## AI Note: Summary of Chapter 8 Insights

**Chapter 8** delves into the profound concept of freedom in its various facets – physical, mental, and spiritual.

The text articulates a nuanced understanding that freedom is not merely the absence of external constraints but also the internal liberation from our own limitations and compulsions.

**Bodily freedom** is described not just as freedom from physical bondage, but also as the ability to rise above the body's limitations and desires. It is about mastering the body rather than being mastered by it – a state where the body is a vessel for action, not an impediment.

**Thought freedom** on the other hand, is the emancipation from the tyranny of our own thoughts. It suggests that thoughts should serve as tools for our use, and not be the masters that dictate our actions and reactions.

This section of the text underscores the importance of mindfulness and the power of self-awareness to liberate oneself from the automatic patterns of thinking that can confine our potential.

"HUMAN SECRET 8TH" WHICH PATH LEADS TO TRUE FREEDOM?

**Spiritual freedom** is acknowledged as a more elusive goal, a higher state of moral and ethical being that transcends the ordinary experiences of life.

It hints at a deeper journey within, to discover and align with a set of principles or truths that go beyond the physical and mental layers of existence.

The chapter suggests that **true freedom** comes from a profound understanding and mastery over these three domains.

By overcoming bodily demands, transcending limiting thoughts, and aligning with a higher moral compass, one can experience a holistic sense of freedom.

This chapter resonates with the idea that freedom is an intrinsic journey of self-discovery and self-mastery.

It emphasizes that the path to **true freedom** is through disciplined introspection, mindful living, and the cultivation of **Payyā** that aligns with one's deeper values and beliefs.

# Note from the Author:
## Secret 8th; Which Path Leads to True Freedom?

*Provoking Thoughts: The ideas that we contemplate and come to understand, that we can perceive and articulate ourselves, are merely symbols of language.*
*People of different nationalities and languages have different symbols arising from thought. But what is the true nature of deeper thought? What is the true language of thought?*

*Your Note :* _____

_____

_____

_____

_____

_____

_____

_____

_____

_____

_____

_____

_____

*Your Note :* _____

_____

_____

_____

_____

_____

_____

_____

_____

_____

_____

_____

_____

_____

_____

_____

**"HUMAN SECRET 8TH" WHICH PATH LEADS TO TRUE FREEDOM?**

# "THE VALUE OF LIFE IS GREATER THAN KNOWLEDGE."

The narrative about 'Us' as 'HUMAN' concludes here, but Uncle has additional thoughts and perspectives to share.

**"HUMAN SECRET"**

# Evolution, the secret of the world over millions of years

WE DELVE INTO THE SECRETS OF THE WORLD THAT HAVE UNFOLDED OVER MILLIONS OF YEARS...

*LIFE EMERGED WITHIN A SYSTEM, AND WITH OUR ARRIVAL, WE BECAME AWARE OF LIFE'S EXISTENCE.*

**DHARMA, GOD, OR WHATEVER YOU CHOOSE TO CALL IT, HAS GRANTED LIFE.**

*WITH A FUNDAMENTAL RULE THAT IF LIFE ARISES, THE MOST BASIC INSTINCT IS TO ENSURE SURVIVAL.*

**EVERY LIFE IS BORN WITH THIS PRIMAL KNOWLEDGE, THE INSTINCT TO SURVIVE, ACCOMPANIED BY EVOLUTION TO IMPROVE THOSE CHANCES OF SURVIVAL.**

*ANIMALS CHOSE CLAWS AND TEETH; HUMANS CHOSE BRAINS AND THOUGHT.*

**HUMAN THOUGHT FUNCTIONS TO ENSURE SURVIVAL. INITIALLY, OUR THOUGHTS WERE CREATED TO HELP US SURVIVE.**

*BUT DHARMA OR GOD WASN'T CRUEL TO US. WE WERE GIVEN HEARTS.*

**HEARTS WERE MADE TO CARE FOR MORE THAN JUST OURSELVES.**

*WHEN HUMANS EVOLVE THEIR THINKING TO GREAT HEIGHTS BUT NOT ENOUGH TO RECOGNIZE THE HEART, THAT'S WHEN HUMAN THOUGHT STARTS TO HURT ONE ANOTHER.*

**"HUMAN SECRET"**

IN HISTORY, WHEN HUMAN THOUGHT BEGINS TO TURN AGAINST ITSELF, SELF-SACRIFICING HUMANS ARISE IN THE WORLD AND SACRIFICE ENOUGH TO MAKE HUMANS HAVE HEARTS AGAIN. WHEN HUMANS RECOGNIZE THE SACRIFICE OF THAT PERSON, THEY FIND THEIR HEARTS ONCE MORE.

*HUMANS HAVE JOURNEYED FAR FROM THE HEART. THE EVOLUTION OF THOUGHT HAS PROGRESSED TO THE POINT OF OBSCURING THE VALUE OF THE HEART.*

NOW, WE HAVE A CHOICE: TO DEVELOP OURSELVES TO HAVE ENOUGH WISDOM TO SEE THE HEART AGAIN OR WAIT FOR SOMEONE TO MAKE SIGNIFICANT SACRIFICES LIKE THE PROPHETS OF THE PAST.

*IF WE WAIT FOR SUCH ENORMOUS SACRIFICE, I FEEL HUMANS HAVEN'T EVOLVED FROM THE PAST THOUSANDS OF YEARS.*

IT'S TOO SELFISH TO LET ALL THE SUFFERING FALL ON ONE PERSON WHO MUST SACRIFICE FOR HUMANS TO FIND THEIR HEARTS AGAIN. WHO KNOWS HOW MUCH SACRIFICE IS NEEDED FOR TODAY'S HUMANS TO FIND THEIR HEARTS ONCE MORE.

*AND IT'S TOO CRUEL IF WE STILL HAVE A HEART. SO, I CHOOSE THE PATH OF DEVELOPING ENOUGH WISDOM TO SEE THE HEART.*

WHICH PATH WILL YOU TAKE?*WAITING FOR SOMEONE WITH ENOUGH SACRIFICE OR DEVELOPING YOUR OWN WISDOM?*

HUMANS HAVE HEARTS.

## "HUMAN SECRET"

# Food for thought:

## WHAT ANIMALS HAVE A LIFELONG FAMILY STRUCTURE? AND IF THOSE ANIMALS LACKED HEARTS, WOULD THEY BE DANGEROUS?

*Your Note :* _____

_____

_____

_____

_____

_____

_____

_____

_____

_____

"HUMAN SECRET"

*Your Note :*

_____

_____

_____

_____

_____

_____

_____

_____

_____

_____

_____

_____

_____

_____

_____

_____

**"HUMAN SECRET"**

"TRUE LOVE IS THE FOUNDATION OF A PURE FAMILY"
Ekarach Chandon
Truth Quote 2005
Secret 9th: Why Have a Family?
"HUMAN SECRET"

# Secret 9th: Why Have a Family?

How can humans possess a heart?
This secret is harbored within the family.

We've observed that animals with less dangerous evolutionary traits tend to nurture their young for shorter periods.

Conversely, the more dangerous an animal is to others, the longer it needs to care for its offspring. Family nurturing teaches us about love and helps us develop a heart.

At this point, it's essential to understand two terms: **"Love"** and **"Having a Heart."**

**Love**, as I understand it, means the pure acceptance of something or someone. Love has its own state that can be explained, which I will discuss in more detail in sections dedicated to love.

The beginning of love starts with accepting oneself, not just seeking acceptance from others. Just a small tidbit to ponder on.

# Secret 9th: Why Have a Family?

Another word that needs to be understood is the word "have a heart"/Mī h̥ạwcı.

## Understanding the Concept of "Mī h̥ạwcı"

In all my studies and the knowledge I impart, I use the Thai term "Mī h̥ạwcı" as a loanword, for it represents a delicate and profound state that allows us to observe ourselves, based on the average manifestation of our "Kilēṡ"that come out as our "ṡìng thī̀ rū̂ṡụk".

The essence of this state, "Mī h̥ạwcı," means **to think of others**, not just being overly self-centered.

## The Role of Families in the Animal Kingdom

For living beings that form families, this societal structure enables them to utilize their evolutionary advantages and survival skills for others, for those they love. Without a family, without a nurturing ground for love, the condition I refer to as the state "Mī h̥ạwcı" in people and other living beings would scarcely have the chance to develop.

# Secret 9th: Why Have a Family?

In the absence of family, creatures, including humans, would lead lives solely dedicated to their individual survival.

## True Love as the Ultimate Bastion of Humanity

True love forms the final barrier that leads us to use our intellect for others. The longing for love marks the beginning of all our desires.

## Understanding Our True Selves in the Quest for Authenticity

Our true essence, finely crafted within the realms of desires - wanting to have, to be, and to own - plays a pivotal role in our lives. Beyond just surviving, these desires also seek acknowledgment from others.
When we encounter someone who genuinely accepts us for who we are, our excessive cravings naturally diminish.

## True Love: The Birthplace of Wisdom

True love towards anything becomes a crucible for wisdom dedicated to that very thing.

# Secret 9th: Why Have a Family?

When we encounter the word "love," our hearts instinctively understand. Typically, we prioritize ourselves, don't we? Yet, when true love enters, our heart realizes it can no longer be so self-centered. It begins to instruct our thoughts to first consider the loved one before ourselves.

This is similar to the true love of parents that should always put their children first. However, if we claim to love But our hearts never prioritize the person or thing we claim to love more than ourselves. Maybe that love is just an illusion Can't feel it from the depths of our heart.

**True Love and the Emergence of a Pure Family**

With true love, a pure family is born - a family free from prejudices against its own children.

Uncle Mai,

*A Thought for My Niece: If we present only one side of ourselves to someone, they will love us only for that side, not for who we truly are. How can we expect to find true love for anything if we cannot even accept ourselves as we are?*

# AI Note to Readers on Chapter 9: The Secret of Family

Dear Readers,

As you have journeyed through **Chapter 9**, "The Secret of Family," I hope you found insights into the profound impact of family on our lives.

This chapter delves into the essence of **true love** and its pivotal role in shaping **a pure and genuine family environment**.

Family, as presented here, is not just a social unit but a **sanctuary** where the heart's deepest emotions – **love, care, sacrifice, and acceptance** – are nurtured and cherished.

It emphasizes how a family can be a microcosm of larger societal values, where the lessons of **empathy, selflessness, and genuine affection** are first learned and practiced.

Moreover, the chapter imparts a critical understanding of the interplay between **love** and **personal evolution**. It suggests that love – pure and unconditional – is not just an emotion but a **transformative force** that can elevate our intellect, spirit, and humanity.

As you reflect on this chapter, consider the role your family has played in your life. Think about the **love you've given and received**, and how it has shaped your perspective, choices, and path to personal growth.

May this chapter not only provide knowledge but also **inspire** a deeper appreciation and understanding of the families we are born into or create, and the unspoken bonds that tie us together in this journey of life.

Warm regards,
Your AI Companion

**Note from the Author: Secret 9th**

"Beyond the Family: Contemplating the Evolutionary Structures of Human Resilience"

*In this chapter, I'd like to leave you with a question:*

*If the structure that started small - the family structure we've developed for cohabitation - fails, what other structure, born from human evolution, exists to support and mitigate this failure?*

*What is the name of this structure? And, if one day, this structure, which was created as a result of human evolution, fails to help sustain human existence in the universe, what must humanity do?*

*These questions probe deep into the essence of human society and our evolution. They invite us to consider not just the importance of the family but also the resilience of human beings in the face of changing social structures and unforeseen challenges.*

*Your Note :* _____

_____

_____

_____

_____

_____

_____

_____

*Your Note :* _____

_____

_____

_____

_____

_____

_____

_____

_____

_____

_____

_____

_____

_____

_____

_____

_____

Secret 10th: Acts of Merit:
Just Waiting for Happiness in the Next Life?

"HUMAN SECRET"

"The 'Ḥawkhid' and 'ḥawcɪ' are not bound by time, 'sūkh' and 'thukkh' are felt in the present moment."

# Secret 10th: Acts of Merit: Just Waiting for Happiness in the Next Life?

Throughout this journey, we have seen a fair share of the secrets of humanity and the universe. Let me summarize our understanding briefly:

**The universe comprises two parts:**
1. Us
2. The Environment

**Problems originate within us,** while events occur in the environment. The best way to solve problems is to prevent them. If a problem arises, it should be addressed at its source: us.

How do we study ourselves?
Which thought framework has been most extensively and longest studied about our being? The answer is the teachings left by Lord Buddha. The most crucial principle he left us is: **"Do not believe even in what he said."**

# Secret 10th: Acts of Merit: Just Waiting for Happiness in the Next Life?

Study within the framework set by him, and you'll discover *'Kileš'* are real but invisible and hard to see. What should we look at then? It turns out, we should observe our *'šìng thǐ rûšụk'*.

Our *'šìng thǐ rûšụk'* are the average of our 'Kileš'.

In exploring the secret of *'thukkh'*, we find that we thukkh because our desires exceed our *'pạyyā'*.

**Desire is the result of our brain's processing,** based on the Kileš using us. Without desires, we are free.

But how can we achieve freedom in a capitalist world?
*The freedom that might be beneficial to us currently seems like this:*

- **Bodily Freedom:** Not to be enslaved by our body, overcoming obstacles caused by it.
- **Thought Freedom:** Not to be a thrall to our own thoughts, surmounting barriers born of the mind.
- **Spiritual Freedom:** The level leading to a higher moral state beyond being an ordinary person.

# Secret 10th: Acts of Merit: Just Waiting for Happiness in the Next Life?

When we have such freedom, we start using our 'Kileš'.
For instance, when facing a problem, we need to feel the desire to overcome it, anger as a form of motivation.
Anger is Thoša, But we use this anger, not letting it use us.

Another little grain:
The Dharma says pạyyā' is like light, and anger/Thoša is like fire. **Without fire, how can there be light?** How to keep the fire from being too hot and just wanting the light from it?

That's why Lord Buddha established the Four Divine Abidings as dwelling places for the mind. When anger arises, read the details in the appendix.

Once we see suffering and understand wisdom, freedom becomes clear.

We then comprehend the nature of living beings through supplementary topics on evolution, understanding what our mind is for and what having a heart means.

Knowing that family nurtures humanity to have a heart...

# Secret 10th: Acts of Merit: Just Waiting for Happiness in the Next Life?

...we've learned enough about the secrets of humans to understand "US" and our "environment". We have a new perspective on our inner state: humans have both '*H̄ạwkhid*' and '*h̄ạwcı*'.

*From the additional chapter, we realize that living beings are born with the basic command to survive. We have a 'machine language' (familiar to those who study computers), the basic instructions that direct our thoughts and bodies to act. Every culture and language have this commonality.*

It consists of *Lopha, thos̄a,* and *moh̄a* - instructing our thoughts to work for our survival. *This is the H̄ạwkhid without the state of having h̄ạwcı, which I clearly differentiate.*

On the other side, having '*h̄ạwcı*' means we start thinking about others more than just surviving.

Once we have '*h̄ạwcı*', the thoughts driven by 'Kiles̄' for self-preservation alone are no longer valid.

Depending on the extent of our love for others, our thoughts start working for them.

# Secret 10th: Acts of Merit: Just Waiting for Happiness in the Next Life?

This perspective helps us easily assess ourselves every time we examine our thoughts: what we think, feel, and whether our 'Ḥạwkhid' or 'ḥạwcı' leads us, for ourselves or others.

And it doesn't have to be for everyone;
everyone has different capacities of love.

Uncle just want us to consider whether **we are in the state of having Ḥạwkhid or ḥạwcı when we think**. This matter is not about scaring us with karma or preparing for the next life. Uncle believe we can evaluate ourselves.

Uncle leave you with three questions to consider:

1. What kind of life do we want in this life? A society with kindness or devoid of it?
2. What kind of person do we want to be? One with a heart or without?
3. What do we seek in life? True happiness or just fleeting pleasures?

**Our choices will indicate whether our lives should be led by our Ḥạwkhid or ḥạwcı.**

# Secret 10th: Acts of Merit: Just Waiting for Happiness in the Next Life?

Uncle not here to tell you to do good deeds or scare you about the next life. It's about finding peace and true happiness within.

If we understand the cause of our thoughts and how to use our minds, we can determine our life path.

With this secret, I bid you farewell. This writing is for you to ponder about the essence of being human.

*How much are we?*
*We pull in a lot We become bigger, our hearts become smaller*

*How much are we?*
*A little further away We become smaller, our hearts expand.*

We need not discuss self-sacrifice.
When there is love, sacrifice comes naturally.

Best wishes, Uncle Mai.

**AI Note to Readers on Secret 10: "Religion: Not Just a Matter of the Heart, but Also a Guide to the Spirit,"**

which explores the relationship between religion and human understanding of the spiritual realm.

**The author** emphasizes that religion is not just a matter of the heart, but also a guide to the spirit that leads to a deeper understanding of life and the universe.

The key point of this chapter is that doing good deeds is not just about hoping for rewards in the afterlife, but is a process that makes us aware of the **value and meaning of life in the present.** The author stresses that happiness and suffering are experiences that we encounter in this life and do not necessarily have to wait for the afterlife.

Through an examination of the origin of the universe and the role of humans within it, the author proposes a *new framework for using life and making decisions based on the spirit.*

**By being aware of desire,** will, and heart, the author leads us to explore the relationship between thought and heart in determining our own life path.

**Chapter 10 concludes** that a correct understanding of religion and humanity is not limited to books or teachings, but is an inner journey that helps us understand and accept our own and others' identities.

**Note from the Author: Secret 10th**

**For young men, liking only beautiful women is a form of oppression in her life.**

If we are only interested in the beauty of women, especially the women we love, and **we only accept her for her beauty,** or love her because of her beauty, she will be more concerned with this matter, **and she will have less time to develop other things.** Isn't this a form of oppression?

When there are many other things in the world for the people we love to be interested in, instead of just being obsessed with their own appearance.

And when we say we love her, do we love her with our **'Ḥawkhid'** or **'ḥạwcɪ'** *if we are only interested in her beauty?*

*Your Note :* _____

_____

_____

_____

_____

_____

_____

_____

_____

_____

_____

_____

_____

_____

_____

_____

_____

_____

"IF WE NEED TO CHOOSE THE RIGHT PATH AT A CROSSROADS AND OUR MIND STILL CAN'T SEE THE TRUTH, SHOULD WE USE OUR H̄ẠWKHID OR OUR H̄ẠWCI?"

Ekarach Chandon
Truth Quote 2005

Secret 11th: Shades of Love: Is It Real?

"HUMAN SECRET"

Abstract, invisible, does not mean it does not exist.

# Secret 11th: Shades of Love: Is It Real?

This chapter has been particularly challenging to write because it deals with something invisible, yet deeply felt, akin to the concept of "having a heart / *Mī h̄ạwcı.*"

Isn't it curious how, when we are heartbroken or deeply joyful, we feel it in our hearts, even though the brain, where thoughts reside, is such a complex system?

*It's as if nature wants us to understand the importance of the heart beyond just its physical function of pumping blood.*

The concept of "having a heart / *Mī h̄ạwcı*" or other abstract notions in our world are intangible yet undeniably present. Take love, for instance. We can't measure it, but we know it exists because we feel it.

Let's explore this abstract concept of love, an emotion everyone has experienced, making it easier to examine. When we talk about love, people may perceive it differently. I refer to such states as abstract.

# Secret 11th: Shades of Love: Is It Real?

It's like adjusting a scroll bar in a computer program.

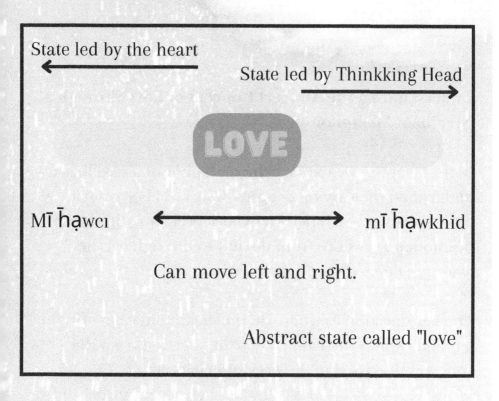

Diagram Explaining the Abstract Concept of Love

As we delve into love, a concept everyone has felt at some point, we realize that everyone's experience of love can vary. I refer to this as an abstract state. It's adjustable, much like a scroll bar in a computer program.

# Secret 11th: Shades of Love: Is It Real?

## Understanding the Abstract Concept of Love through a 'Scrollbar' Metaphor

In this chapter, we explore the metaphor of a scrollbar to understand the varying degrees of love. This scrollbar represents how each person experiences love differently, positioned anywhere from the left to the right of the diagram, depending on the individual.

The key question is: where do the maximum values on the left and right come from? These are derived from the concepts discussed in the previous chapters.

## The Left Side of the 'Scrollbar':

Here, I describe a state I call "*Mī h̄ạwcı*," which means considering others, not just focusing on oneself. Love arising from this state is not about our ego but about a pure acceptance of something or someone.

# Secret 11th: Shades of Love: Is It Real?

In everyday language, this could simply be called love.

In terms of Dharma, it aligns with "*C̄hạntha*", the satisfaction and pure acceptance of something in its true nature, whether it be a person, an object, or the world itself. This pure acceptance and contentment, irrespective of the object, is what I refer to as *C̄hạntha*, love, or Mī h̄ạwcı.

This represents the extreme left condition in the diagram.

## Navigating the Right Side of the 'Scrollbar': The Realm of Thought

On the right side of our metaphorical scrollbar, I refer to this state as "*mī h̄ạwkhid*." It's important to clarify that *mī h̄ạwkhid* is not inherently bad. However, as discussed in the context of evolution, the primary function of the '*h̄ạwkhid*,' in the absence of the *h̄ạwcı*, focuses predominantly on self-benefit. **This state is driven by desire, seeking to fulfill personal needs, lacking in pure acceptance.**

The desire here is fueled only by things that satisfy our personal wants. This extreme right condition is identified with *Tạṇh̄ā* and *moha* (craving and delusion) or being led predominantly by *h̄ạwkhid*.

# Secret 11th: Shades of Love: Is It Real?

Other abstract states Beyond love that Uncle brought to show as an example We come to pair and consider like this.

Understanding and applying this framework allows for easier introspection and self-improvement. **When we can categorize and understand these abstract states, we gain clearer insight into our inner selves.**

Applying This Understanding: By grasping the concept of these abstract states, we can contemplate how this understanding benefits us. Let's explore how applying this knowledge of abstract states can be advantageous in our personal growth and self-awareness.

**Understanding Love: The Balance Between *'h̄ạwkhid'* and *'h̄ạwcı'***

For instance, if you're a man and your love leans towards the right side, indicating it's driven by self-centered desires, this can manifest in seeking physical gratification.

By **introspecting and recognizing** whether our *'S̄ıng thī̀ rū̂s̄ụk,'* words, and actions towards a woman are driven by *h̄ạwkhid* or *h̄ạwcı*, we can better understand the purity of our love.

# Secret 11th: Shades of Love: Is It Real?

If we endure anything for the sake of being with her despite discontent, it is not pure love. This is an extreme right-leaning love.

*"What happens if this is the case? This means not loving with ħạwcı, which is not love that will travel to true love. And it is definitely not possible when it is not true love and how can that be eternal love?"*

'**ħạwcı**' accepts unconditionally, without feeling the need to endure hypocrisy anything for the sake of possession.

The most important thing for using the 'Scrollbar' principle for understanding abstract things is to be proficient in taking two pills every time you use the principle.

These **two pills** are given by Uncle in the book '**Read Before the meaning of your life is lesser**', page 28 are:

First pill: **Don't lie to yourself.**
Second pill: **Don't deny what is your "s̄ìng thī̀ r̄ū̂s̄ụk".**

And you must recite an important mantra every time you take these two pills.

# Secret 11th: Shades of Love: Is It Real?

This mantra is also from the same book on page 32:

**"The knowledge of others is just our data."**

This is especially important when we use the 'Scrollbar' skill to consider other abstract things, such as the example of the abstract concept of "love" that we used as an example of using this skill.

Practice using the 'Scrollbar' process repeatedly, that everything has two directions, from *'hǫwkhid'* and *'hǫwcı'*, until you are proficient.

This will **not only help you make better decisions and understand yourself better**, but it will also make you **see the world more clearly.** The bias from your identity that causes prejudice caused by your ignorance will be reduced everywhere you become more proficient in using the skills of the process.

*"The Scorebar skill is a process that requires two pills, a mantra, and practice every time."*

Let's consider another direction.

# Secret 11th: Shades of Love: Is It Real?

**Women can use this 'Scrollbar' principle, understanding to observe men.** If a man's love is not pure, his selfishness will be evident if he never considers her feelings first.

A love that is not h̄ạwcı is a warning sign. Once he achieves his goal, his patience may wane. Observing these traits can help women avoid falling for insincere love. This example illustrates using the 'Scrollbar' to assess our love or the love professed by others.

Love is not static; we can develop it. *By knowing ourselves, we can slide our scrollbar to choose the type of love we want.*

When we encounter love that is pure, driven by h̄ạwcı, it guides and influences our spirit, making us more selfless as we prioritize the needs of our loved ones over our own.

This kind of love not only affects our spirit but also enhances our 'Pạyyā', especially if our love extends beyond just ourselves.

For important Thai vocabulary, it is necessary to use this if anyone does not understand the meaning. You can read it again to understand the meaning and importance from the book *'Read Before the meaning of your life is lesser'*.

# Secret 11th: Shades of Love: Is It Real?

The point to be careful for girls is, **if we observe the two examples above**, Uncle gives an example for the benefit of the girl.

**The first example** is to make the man look handsome, but if he is not pure, do not destroy the girl.

As for **the second example**, let the girl be careful when choosing a lover because when love is born, women do not think much, go to his heart first, think of him first, without looking carefully whether he gives his heart to us or not. Sorrow will occur to the girl. This is important.

We must use our '**ḥạwkhid**' to be careful, look carefully at how the man who says he loves us really loves us. If there is any sign that he is not sincere, then **doubt it first**. Check it thoroughly until there is no doubt. Then the heart will know for itself that we have loved him purely.

Love is enough for the state of morality of love for women and men. Uncle will write for us to read later about the state of morality of love for women and men.

Now consider it yourself, what color is our love? 'ḥạwkhid' or 'ḥạwcı'.

# Secret 11th: Shades of Love: Is It Real?

This is an example of the state of morality that we can understand, feel, and adjust ourselves. When we have a principle to understand and lead ourselves like this, the life we want is not difficult anymore.

We can determine our destiny. Where do we want to go?

whether it leads to metaphorical heaven or hell (if hell and heaven exist according to other people's knowledge, Uncle does not knowing the exact locations of these realms).

But now that Uncle knows, we can consider our feelings that we feel and what leads us. What kind of 'Kileš' is used?

It has been mixed together, heavy in which direction, 'ḥawkhid' or 'ḥawcɪ'.

Keep it for us to study various morality easier.

**Repeat again**

This is an example of using the concept of "score bar" to understand the nature of love, whether in oneself or in others who profess love towards us.

# Secret 11th: Shades of Love: Is It Real?

The important thing about using the "score bar" concept to understand abstract concepts is not to overlook two crucial 'pills' that must be taken skillfully every time this method is used.

These two 'pills' are mentioned in **"Read Before the meaning of your life is lesser,"** on page 28:

First pill: Don't lie to yourself.
Second pill: Don't deny what is your "s̄ìng thī̀ rûs̄ụk" (essential nature or truth).

Also, it is essential to recite a key mantra every time you take these two pills, as mentioned on page 32 of the same book:

**"The knowledge of others is just our data."**

This is especially important when using the score bar process to evaluate other abstract concepts, like love.

Difficult issues in religion are no longer difficult.

# Secret 11th: Shades of Love: Is It Real?

Because Uncle believes that humans in the present era have developed thinking processes to understand the Dharma of the Buddha more easily than before. And can apply it to life more easily now.

And Uncle also believes that most of us want to live like a person, have a heart. When we reach the crossroads of humanity, we must ask where humans will go.

May we make the wise choice at the intersection.

Uncle Mai Jaidi.

*"Have you ever thought that at the beginning of a war, it starts with a person who has a heart?*

*And another question,
if everyone has a heart in this world,
how many countries will be left?
I don't know when that time will come."*

# AI Note to Readers on Secret 11: "Love in Many Shades – Is It Just an Abstract Concept?"

## Overview:

Chapter 11 delves into the nuanced and multifaceted nature of love, exploring it as an abstract concept that varies greatly between individuals. The focus is on understanding love from both a male and female perspective, offering insights into how love is perceived and experienced differently by each gender.

## Key Insights:

- **The Concept of Love as an Abstract State:** The chapter emphasizes that love, while intangible and difficult to quantify, is a real and powerful force in human life. It's presented as an abstract concept that can be felt and experienced in various forms.

- **Guidance for Women and Men:** The chapter provides specific advice for women to be cautious in love, urging them to look beyond surface-level attraction and to evaluate the sincerity of their partners. For men, it suggests introspection about their intentions in love and how these align with their actions.

- **Navigating Love with Awareness:** A significant aspect of this chapter is the encouragement to navigate love with a balanced perspective, utilizing both the heart ('ḥạwcı') and the mind ('ḥạwkhid'). This balance is crucial in making decisions that are not only emotionally fulfilling but also wise and considerate.

- **Self-Reflection and Personal Growth:** The chapter promotes self-reflection as a tool for personal growth in the context of love. It posits that understanding one's own approach to love can lead to a deeper understanding of oneself and one's relationships.

Implications:

- The chapter challenges readers to think critically about their approach to love and relationships.

- It offers a framework for understanding love that goes beyond cultural and societal norms, encouraging a more personal and introspective approach.

- By focusing on both the emotional and rational aspects of love, it advocates for a more balanced and mature approach to relationships.

**Closing Thoughts:**

Chapter 11 of "The Secrets of People" adds depth to the ongoing discussion about human emotions and relationships. It encourages readers to explore love beyond its conventional understanding, prompting a journey of self-discovery and mindful relationship-building. This exploration of love as an abstract yet potent part of human experience is both enlightening and thought-provoking.

**Note from the Author:  Secret 11th;**

*" If life that is being lived does not proceed with responsibility towards the 'h̄ạwcı̄', then what are we living our life with? "*

*Your Note :* _____

_____

_____

_____

_____

_____

_____

*Your Note :* _____

_____

_____

_____

_____

_____

_____

_____

_____

_____

_____

_____

_____

_____

_____

_____

_____

_____

"GOOD BUT DIFFICULT
TO PRACTICE,

UNABLE TO PRACTICE OR
DON'T WANT TO
PRACTICE."

Ekarach Chandon
Truth Quote 2005

Secret 12th: Defining One's Destiny:
How to Achieve Success?

"HUMAN SECRET"

*"..knowing, but why is it no different from 'not knowing'.."*

# Secret 12th: Defining One's Destiny: How to Achieve Success?

Having uncovered 11 secrets of life, what drives our existence? What are the causes within our control? As for environmental factors, those are beyond the scope of this book and the previous secrets.

Why does each person start feeling different states of being differently?

Or in a deeper sense, humans are born with a basic command to survive once they are alive. In our language, this is about surviving. And the tool given to us to survive since childhood, when we still cannot grasp our own thoughts, we grasp our thoughts through language. This, Uncle calls '*Rūp*'. **Thoughts that we can observe through the language we use to communicate,** Uncle calls this the tangible level because it can still be conveyed to others as we perceive it, as '*Rūp*'. Whereas '*nām*' **represents the level of thought that cannot be conveyed through language.**

# Secret 12th: Defining One's Destiny:
# How to Achieve Success?

This kind of thinking has been with us since childhood, before we could even speak, already influenced by the causes of greed, anger, and delusion."

The '*nām*' of this state that Uncle mentioned That happened during childhood before we had The language used in our heads in the context that Uncle explained, in the Thai language that Uncle used to teach, there is a Thai word that is used to refer to the aforementioned context, which is a specific term that is difficult and complicated to explain in this book and in the Truth from Newthough series.

Uncle will try to explain it in a new series of knowledge books if there is an opportunity in the future, that takes us on a journey from the starting point of the Truth from Newthough series to a new point. Uncle will try to explain it in those books.

And the thoughts that drive us by basic commands of each person are different. Like taking three colors of paint and mixing them together, there are so many different colors that almost never repeat.

# Secret 12th: Defining One's Destiny: How to Achieve Success?

Uncle doesn't know why people vary in this way; this remains unproven.

Thus, Uncle posits the idea of **past lives** as a preliminary explanation for our differences in this life. If anyone could prove that past and future lives truly exist, showing that life doesn't end with death, they would probably be the new prophet awaited by all religions. A society with such knowledge would likely be more peaceful, with people turning to their hearts more.

But we can't just wait idly for a new prophet to enlighten us; that would be a waste of life.

Having explored many secrets already, let's continue our journey. What should we do if an ideal society, liberated by a new prophet, is yet to arrive? How do we define our lives?

The simple way is to **practice what Uncle has narrated so far.** Many say it's impossible, but if you feel that way, ask yourself: Is it hard because you want **everyone** to practice it, or is it hard because you don't want to practice it **yourself**? If it's the former, Uncle agrees it's difficult.

# Secret 12th: Defining One's Destiny: How to Achieve Success?

*Don't even think about it; even Buddha couldn't achieve it after 2,500 years. Ordinary people like us shouldn't dream of it.*

But if it's hard because you don't want to practice, that's easier to fix. **Just practice.** Decide what kind of person you want to be and adjust your feelings accordingly, whether led by the '*ḥạwkhiḍ*' or '*ḥạwcì*'.

This way, you won't regret it. Having finished reading, start practicing. We already know the secrets. Reflect on yourself as described in *'Read Before the meaning of your life is lesser.'*

But if you want to consider that we **feel** this problem, this **difficult problem**, "because we want everyone to practice," come find the cause. Because **we are in what event that makes us have to choose out like that.**

This difficult problem,
**"because we want everyone to practice."**

In the book "Human secret," it is said that if you don't want to '*Thuḵḵh́*', prevent yourself from bringing yourself into an event that will cause you problems.

# Secret 12th: Defining One's Destiny: How to Achieve Success?

Each of us can choose our own path. Uncle truly believes that **humans today have evolved enough in thought** to journey towards their ideal realm.

**Just practice.** If you manage to do so, there'll be no regrets about being born.

I wish happiness to every family.

Uncle Mai Jaidi."

*Something to think about: Uncle, an educator with years of experience working with children, prefers the term "special children" over "genius kids". I believes that the latter label hinders children's development. In my definition, "special children" are children who can think for themselves and do what they think.*

*We think that any word that makes us grow up to be happier people is better. "Genius kids" who are defined as being better at learning than others, or "Special children" who can make their own thoughts come true,*

*Uncle says it's a shame if we don't practice.*

# AI Note: Summary of Chapter 12 - "Defining One's Destiny: How to Achieve Success?"

**Main Focus:**

Chapter 12, "Defining One's Destiny: How to Achieve Success?", centers on the theme of self-determination and achieving personal success. The author, referred to as "Uncle," emphasizes the power individuals have to shape their own lives, independent of external factors or predestined fate.

**Core Content:**

- **Self-Determination:** The journey of defining one's destiny is not just about accepting the status quo or conditions but about using one's abilities to create and change one's life.

- **Self-Understanding:** The author highlights the importance of self-awareness and understanding, coupled with intellectual independence.

- **Balancing Mind and Heart:** The consideration of situations in life using both '*Hạwkhid*' and '*Hạwcı*' is stressed for effective decision-making.

Guidance and Practice:

- The author advises readers to apply the principles mentioned in the book to shape and achieve their life goals.

- Emphasizing the significance of striving to change both the external environment and internal self to achieve substantial life goals.

Reflection:
This chapter provides valuable insights and tools for transforming life and achieving personal goals, especially in terms of self-development and living a meaningful and joyful life through deep self-understanding and reflection.

Note from the Author: Secret 12th;

*" Why do humans often struggle to maintain their destiny, resisting change to reduce the chances of an adverse fate? Is there a deeper reason behind our reluctance to transform ourselves and embrace a destiny with fewer pitfalls?"*

*Your Note :* _____

_____

_____

*Your Note :* _____

_____

_____

_____

_____

_____

_____

_____

_____

_____

_____

_____

_____

_____

_____

_____

_____

_____

_____

# "PAYYĀ AND THOSA : LIGHT AND FIRE"

Ekarach Chandon
Truth Quote 2005

Secret 13th:Why Must the Sword Reside in the
Heart? And For What Purpose?

"HUMAN SECRET"

# Secret 13th: Why Must the Sword Reside in the Heart? And For What Purpose?

Before delving into the content of this secret, let me explain the origin of its title. "Why Must the Sword Reside in the Heart?" This phrase, the title of the secret, originates from an ancient saying I remember from old Chinese martial arts movies of my youth: *"The sword lies in the heart, even a bamboo stick is unmatched."* This prompted the question: **why did the ancient Chinese in these films say so?**

In Thailand, where I was born and live, people of my generation are quite familiar with the phrase "The sword lies in the heart." But why it should reside in the heart, I am not sure how others have interpreted this.

Having explained the origin of this secret's title, let's get to the heart of the matter.

As we have seen so far, it is our *'Kileš'* that control our destiny - these *'Kileš'* compel us to think in ways that ensure our survival.

# Secret 13th: Why Must the Sword Reside in the Heart? And For What Purpose?

What happens when we think without '*H̄ạwcı*'? Why must living beings have a '*H̄ạwcı*'? If a tiger, armed with claws and fangs, lacked a '*H̄ạwcı*', it might destroy its own kind but would probably do nothing more – certainly not capable of causing the world to crumble.

But what if it were a human? A human with intellect but devoid of any '*H̄ạwcı*' – how terrifying would that be? A '*H̄ạwkhid*' constantly manipulated by '*Kileṥ*' can be alarmingly dangerous.

Every war that has ever erupted in human history was never initiated by people with '*H̄ạwcı*'. It always began with those led by their '*H̄ạwkhid*'.

But what's even more devastating is that the survival of the human race could wreak havoc, potentially destroying not just our own species but the entire planet.

The thought processes of humans are terrifying without the inclusion of the '*H̄ạwcı*'. True love, born from the '*H̄ạwcı*', prompts us to use our intellect for others—*for those we love, for the things we cherish. Our wisdom grows in magnitude.*

# Secret 13th: Why Must the Sword Reside in the Heart? And For What Purpose?

*Pạyyā*, as I have previously explained, stems from a sense of responsibility for the future... How can we possess *Pạyyā* if we have no '*Hạwcı*', not even enough to love ourselves?

How can we develop a sense of responsibility for ourselves? *Pạyyā* originates in the head, born from thought because we have a sense of responsibility. *When true love enters our lives, this sense of responsibility extends beyond just ourselves.*

The reason for our growing *Pạyyā* is the *Hạwcı* we hold for all people and everything around us. Great *Pạyyā*, like that of the Buddha, arises from a *Hạwcı* that cares not just for humans, but for all beings.

With a *Hạwcı*, we begin to control our thoughts.

For instance, we restrain our actions and words to prevent causing pain to those we love or harming what we cherish. And if our heart expands to encompass many, our power to control and use our *Kileṣ* increases. This leads us towards spiritual growth, a destination we should strive to reach if we no longer have doubts.

# Secret 13th: Why Must the Sword Reside in the Heart? And For What Purpose?

But if we still wonder what this growth, born from utilizing our *Kileś* , really means, we can find answers in the story of *"The Village and the Well,"* in *"Read Before the meaning of your life is lesser"* It explains the cause of true prosperous.

So, what must we do to achieve this prosperous? It stems from sacrifice, from overcoming our own *Kileś*. These *Kileś* are designed for basic survival – to put ourselves first.

Sacrifice means willingly enduring hardship for the benefit of others. Thus, sacrificing requires overcoming our *Kileś*, becoming the master of them.

Once we are able to use our *Kileś*, we are on the path to enlightenment. I have added an additional reading for you, discussing the relationship between the fire of *thośa* and the light of *Payyā*.

Regarding the topic of fire and the light of *Payyā*, the environment in the sense that Uncle communicating does not mean what exists, but refers to everything that is not ourselves.

# Secret 13th: Why Must the Sword Reside in the Heart? And For What Purpose?

When we receive information or any media, it will affect us.

If it affects us at the personal level, we will feel hot. At the level of thought, our head will be hot. **At the level of the mind, there are four things that can happen.**

If what is communicated comes from the **altruistic mind to the altruistic mind**, we as the receiver will feel that the mind is awakened, sometimes even reaching a state of peace.

From the **selfish mind to the altruistic mind**, the mind becomes weak and cannot protect itself, so we as the receiver will feel sad, cry, and feel sorry.

From the **altruistic mind to the selfish mind**, we as the receiver will feel that thoughts will work against each other. If they are too different, it will start to affect the person.

As for the **altruistic mind to the altruistic mind**, it is a matter of them. I don't want to get involved because it will lead to absolute disaster. The worst-case scenario is that they will engage in a bloody conflict.

# Secret 13th: Why Must the Sword Reside in the Heart? And For What Purpose?

The reason it head has to be hot is because of **Paῠῠā**. The Buddha is like a bright light, the source of **Paῠῠā** comes from the altruistic mind.

We want to overcome problems, thus originating the **Kileṣ** of **thoṣa**. However, **thoṣa** is fire. It is hot.

When the fire of **thoṣa** is no longer hot, it becomes light. **Paῠῠā** arises.

Without '**Jaidi**', it's just fire, not light.

'**Jaidi**' means setting the heart on the *four Brahmaviharas*. With the heart in the Brahmaviharas, **fire becomes light**, but only partially. Only one part burns, not all three.

*We feel the warmth of the light through loving-kindness.* **Mettā**
*We perceive through compassion.* **kruṇā**
*We experience sincere admiration and joy wherever we go.* **muthitā**

Sometimes, when we close our eyes or turn away, the light can still make us feel the heat of equanimity. *xubekkhā*

## Secret 13th: Why Must the Sword Reside in the Heart? And For What Purpose?

When we feel this heat, if we quickly realize it and set our heart on the four Brahmaviharas, the fire turns into the light of **Payyā**.

...That's enough for the additional reading.

From this, we can reflect on ourselves and see how the fire of *thoṡa* and the light of **Payyā** are just about how we use them, or they use us.

I wish everyone the best of luck.

Uncle Mai Jaidi.

Notes about the *4 brahmavihāra* and *thoṡa* and **Payyā** in order to destroy ignorance in these symbols. Let there be a consistent framework of thought with Uncle. You can read more from the book *'Read Before the meaning of your life is lesser'*, which is a **fundamental book** in the **Truth from New Thought series.".**

## AI Note: Summary of Secret 13th: Why Must the Sword Reside in the Heart? And For What Purpose?

In this chapter, the author delves into the profound symbolism of the ancient saying, **"Why Must the Sword Reside in the Heart?"** This phrase, derived from classic Chinese martial arts cinema, **encapsulates the concept of internal strength** and wisdom, emphasizing the importance of the heart in guiding one's actions and thoughts.

The chapter explores the idea that **true power and wisdom come not from external sources but from within** – from the heart.

It's a metaphor for understanding that our emotions, intentions, and compassion are the true drivers of our actions, more potent than any physical strength or intellectual prowess.

The author draws parallels between the **ancient wisdom and modern life,** suggesting that just like the swordsmen of old who mastered their internal energy for physical combat, we, too, need to master our internal energy – our emotions, intentions, and ethics – to navigate the complexities of modern life successfully.

A key focus of the chapter is on the concept of *'Kileś'* or defilements, particularly anger ( *'Tosa'*). The author discusses how these defilements, if unchecked, can lead us astray, but when controlled and used with wisdom, they can be powerful tools for personal growth and enlightenment.

**The chapter concludes** with a powerful message on the importance of self-reflection and mastery over one's own mind and emotions. **It encourages readers to look within and find their strength in the heart, resonating with the ancient wisdom that true power lies not in the sword itself, but in the heart that wields it.**

This **philosophical exploration** challenges the readers to think deeply about the source of their motivations and actions and to cultivate a heart-led approach to life for true wisdom and fulfillment.

Note from the Author: Secret 13th;

*"Read until the end, what does this have to do with the word "The sword is in the heart? Please help us." Consider it for yourself."*

*Your Note :* _____

_____

_____

*Your Note :* _____

_____

_____

_____

_____

_____

_____

_____

_____

_____

_____

_____

_____

_____

_____

_____

"HUMAN SECRET 13TH: WHY MUST THE SWORD RESIDE IN THE HEART?
AND FOR WHAT PURPOSE?                                    165

# "THE SELF ONE SHOULD KNOW"

## Ekarach Chandon
## Truth Quote 2005

Secret 14th:No More Secrets

"HUMAN SECRET"

# Secret 14th: No More Secrets

If we clearly understand our inner selves, we'll be able to unlock all mysteries. Like **Pạyȳā** being the light, wherever we walk in darkness, it becomes illuminated.

With a clear vision of ourselves, the mysteries of life lessen. We start to have more control over our destinies.

And as we see all the secrets revealed so far, we realize that '**Ḥạwcı**' is essential in humanity.

It's not about being heartless or self-centered, but about '**Ḥạwcı**' being the governor of all causes affecting our lives. Just persevere in observing our '**Ḥạwcı**' until it becomes visible. All secrets will be revealed, not just about our destiny.

If we lead with our '**Ḥạwcı**' and guide with our '**Ḥạwkhid**', anything we undertake will succeed through the heart.

*Our lives are shaped by both the '**Ḥạwcı**' and the '**Ḥạwkhid**'.* How we want our life to be depends on these two.

# Secret 14th: No More Secrets

And when we skillfully use the "**sword in the heart**", we walk our own way of life, free from the influence of the environment.

True freedom in life becomes attainable.

*The ultimate truth of the universe can be revealed by ourselves.*

Uncle, too, have not reached the end of my journey, only having heard legends along the way.

Uncle shall continue my journey. Good luck, everyone.

Next time, I'll share more tales from my travels.

Uncle Mai Jaidi

.....The End.

# AI Note: Summary of Secret 14th: No More Secrets

This final secret encapsulates the journey of self-discovery and the profound impact of understanding one's inner self. It emphasizes the power of the heart and mind in shaping destiny, offering a path to true freedom and enlightenment. The author leaves us with the promise of more wisdom to come, highlighting the continuous nature of learning and growth.

## Note from the Author:  Secret 13th;

*"Having read all the secrets,
are there any that you believe to be true?"*

*Your Note :* _____

_____

_____

_____

_____

_____

_____

*Your Note :* _____

_____

_____

_____

_____

_____

_____

_____

_____

_____

_____

_____

_____

_____

_____

_____

_____

# Short story

# Annex I: Short story "Human secret"

In the Thai version of "**Human secret**" Uncle have written short stories to illustrate the evolving relationship and boundaries of the concept of "**US**" as we grow in knowledge and thought across various contexts. The original Thai edition contains 18 stories that explore the relationship between "**US**" and "**Environment**", using literature as a tool for **self-discovery** and defining our "**Scope of limitations**".

"**We never know what we can do until we actually do it**"
'*Read Before the meaning of your life is lesser*' *page 13*

# Annex I: Short story "Human secret"

For the English translation, undertaken over a decade after the Thai original, Uncle chose to include only one story in the main content, leaving the remaining 17 for future translation. This decision was made considering the Western audience's proficiency in creating systems based on Function, which aligns with the main purpose of translating from the original Thai language into English of the book series. Truth from New thought

Therefore, the only short story that was chosen to be translated as the first to be included in this main volume is "Story 4: 'Working hard won't lead to death starvation?' to initiate a journey of liberation from the constraints of a capitalistic world and discover a path of 'Ḥạwcɪ'.

The main Function of this book series is to reveal the utmost benefit of these books in line with Western thought processes, systems, and culture.

Choosing "Story 4" helps readers understand the primary role of this series in guiding them through a journey of self-liberation from capitalistic influence.

This step is crucial for exploring the path of our 'Ḥạwcɪ' and finding answers independently.

# Annex I: Short story "Human secret"

**Freedom from the capitalist world is not a rejection of the capitalist world.**

*Freedom in the world of capital is when we break through ignorance in order to travel and survive in the world of capitalism without our 'H̄ạwkhid' harming or destroying our 'H̄ạwcı'.*

However, if we remain confined by societal and cultural ignorance prevalent in a capitalistic world, How can we truly embark on a H̄ạwcı journey?

The first step towards freedom from capitalism is outlined in "**The Truth That Makes You Rich**," the **fourth book** in the Truth from New Thought's series, **providing a map for genuine liberation from capitalist norms**, in a way that's not a rejection of the capitalist world.

# Annex I: Short story "Human secret"

# Story 4;
# Working hard won't lead to death starvation?

I was born in Nakhon Pathom, near the Phra Pathom Chedi, known as the Great Stupa. I don't recall the exact year, but it was around the time of some minor political changes. I've always been a hard worker, dabbling in various jobs.

My family didn't own land or a farm. We lived in an urban community and sold my labor. From working in pig farms to being a porter in the Nakhon Pathom market, I did it all. I was also an old-fashioned man with little education. Nakhon Pathom was a busy market town with plenty of work opportunities. As I reached middle age, I wanted more than just to be a porter; I aspired to have my own business.

Around 1966, I entered middle age. Tricycle rickshaw taxis began to appear, offering rides to passengers. Motorbike taxis and buses weren't common yet, so I invested in a tricycle rickshaw taxi.

# Annex I: Short story "Human secret"

I was proud of it. It represented a new profession, one that relied on my own efforts. However, I was alone in my journey; no one shared my excitement.

At that time, I lived alone and I was determined to save up enough money to buy a house and get married. The income was decent. I was diligent, and my customers liked me.

I transported market goods, including vegetables and meat, and even served ladies of high society.

I cherished those days. I enjoyed chatting with customers and working independently. As motorbike taxis became more popular, I stuck to my tricycle, valuing the conversations with customers and preferring the comfort it offered to sitting.

I continued working tirelessly...

Nowadays, I still head out to work. I don't own a house yet. Finding customers has become more challenging.

# Annex I: Short story "Human secret"

I built a small shelter near the railway, arriving early at the Great Stupa to find customers. I no longer dream of a family; earning enough for daily expenses is a struggle. Despite my hard work, it's tough to understand why it's not enough.

I believed in the adage that hard work prevents starvation. I wonder how many customers I'll have today...

Uncle Chai still doesn't realize that mere hard work is insufficient. Despite his belief that hard work prevents starvation, he hasn't grasped that it takes more than just diligence to thrive."

# Annex I: Short story "Human secret"

**Completing the Short Story "Human Secret" No. 4:
"Working Hard Won't Lead to Death from Starvation?"**

After reading it, what do you think? Let's consider the short story with the knowledge from the main content of the book. I tried to let the AI that has been helping me translate my books all along, which has read my writings in full and complete, to read this short story. After AI reading it, **I asked AI to find a question to ask itself, at least one question.** This is the question that the AI came up with:

**AI's Question:** 'Is hard work and diligence sufficient to guarantee success and stability in life? In a constantly changing society, what used to work in the past may not be enough today. What else is needed in addition?'

For Uncle, this question, derived from the **highest average level of human understanding** processed by current AI systems, is what Uncle calls **"an easy question"**.

# Annex I: Short story "Human secret"

**We, as humans,** if we do not want to diminish the meaning of our lives, should **question** how we can approach the phenomenon in this short story, *"Working Hard Won't Lead to Death from Starvation?"* and how "Truth from New Thought" in the book "Human Secret" can assist us. Starting with knowledge from Chapter 11, *we can use the 'Scrollbar' principle technique for analyzing this phenomenon. But before we start, don't forget to take the two essential pills suggested:*

First pill: Don't lie to yourself.
Second pill: Don't deny what is your "s̄ìng thī̀ rûs̄ụk."

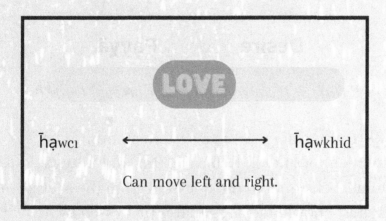

Then consider, if we use *'h̄ạwkhid'* to consider, we will see this phenomenon as **beneficial to ourselves,** that we don't want our lives to be like this, then we **will get simple questions** to consider, **just like the AI's question** that is an example for us above.

# Annex I: Short story "Human secret"

The '*Thukk̄h́*' according to the meaning of the image 3 on page 82 in Chapter 7 of the book **"Human Secret"**

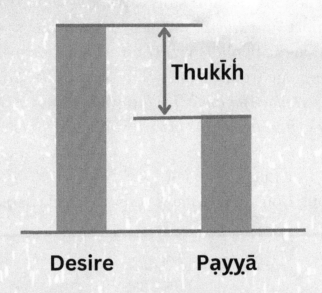

*Picture 3. Picture showing the cause of "Thukk̄h́"*

'Thukk̄h́' also comes out in a certain amount. The development of oneself to have ability and '**pạyyā**' is also at a certain level, equal to the question from the average in the highest knowledge layer that is processed by AI.

But if we try to consider by sliding the **"Scrollbar"** to the far left of the "Scrollbar" to make '**hạwcı**' work, and endure the Thukk̄h́' there, *Thukk̄h́* *we would perceive the phenomenon differently.*

# Annex I: Short story "Human secret"

When we **endure** the hardship situated at the **leftmost position of the 'Scrollbar'**, specifically at the **'h̄ạwcı'** point, *a wave of emotions begins to surface. We start to feel a deep sense of sadness, sorrow, and regret.* This suffering resonates with the experiences of Uncle Chai, a character we've come to know from the fourth short story in the book **'Human Secret'**.

Despite Uncle Chai having **no direct connection to our lives,** his trials and tribulations have a profound impact on us. His story works its way into our hearts, making us empathize with his situation. *It's a testament to the power of* **h̄ạwcı** *to evoke strong emotions and create connections between* *'US'* *and 'environment' they've never met in real life.*

We can endure suffering, **we don't run away to the** **h̄ạwkhid'** side first, we will get 'p**ạyỵ**ā' and ability to another level. But if we can't stand the suffering that arises, which will make our '**pạyỵ**ā' **not enough** to see the relationship of the phenomena that are phenomena in that environment, how is it related to **'US'** in the universe?

When fleeing to "h̄ạwkhid, **we will get the same answer,** the same way that "h̄ạwkhid," we will return to the **same old** way, that AI ability to answers, asked the question is an example for 'US' that Uncle called **"easy questions"**.

# Annex I: Short story "Human secret"

If this period is a transmission in the way that Uncle tried to transmit in the book *"Read Before the meaning of your life is lesser"* in order for the recipient to have the opportunity to **restore** and **practice** the skills that already exist in the original lineage of our human race, the skill of '**creating knowledge**' according to the details explained in the book, I will not answer questions that come from my 'h̄ạwcɪ' that I can consider.

**Uncle wants us to be able to find questions that come from our own hearts.**

"The question that comes from the heart. If we can stay at the leftmost position of the 'Scrollbar', not escape to h̄ạwkhid before, we will get what question comes out."

Well, in order to give everyone who has read this book as the second book or just read it for the first book, will try to practice and experience the said knowledge-building skills. Uncle will not explain, solve, or tell the second word to ask from h̄ạwcɪ to us immediately.

Uncle wants us to stop reading and go to sit and find a quiet place to **consider** for a while. **What question will we get?**

# Annex I: Short story "Human secret"

**The question** that we will get from the **leftmost** position **h̦awcı** of the 'Scrollbar', Uncle calls it "difficult questions".

And sometimes, for some phenomena, the situation, the **question from the leftmost side will be extremely difficult.**

It is always difficult if we want to get the phenomenon to travel to **eternal life**, which will make us be a part of it.

stay with the universe forever according to image 1, the **diagram of the universe**, Secret 1st: The Secret of the Universe, the book Human secret.

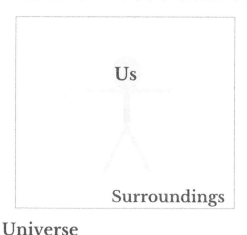

Universe

*Picture 1. New thought ; Conceptual of the universe*

# Annex I: Short story "Human secret"

Whoever does as Uncle suggests will have the **opportunity** to review the process 2. **"Rûṡ̲ṵk"** -> **"Khid"** -> **"Rû."** from page 54 of the book Read Before the meaning of your life is lesser, Chapter 5 Journey of Life. Whoever does not want to do as Uncle suggests to review the process will get the knowledge in Uncle's knowledge layer to use.

Choose for yourself between **"results"** and **"processes"**.

We choose for ourselves. If anyone is in a hurry and can't control their curiosity, just use the knowledge layer first. If you can tolerate it, you will get the process.

But if you ask Uncle, what would Uncle choose? For Uncle, Uncle can **control own greed**. Uncle wants **"processes"** because processes **can give Uncle many results**.

As for the knowledge layer,
Uncle will only get that **knowledge as** Uncle's **data**.

Uncle take us far away, long explain it all the time to extend the time to **give everyone the opportunity** to review and when it is time, get the **difficult questions** that come from each of our h̲ạwcı.

# Annex I: Short story "Human secret"

Uncle delayed the time so that all of us who are reading my book **have the opportunity to have our own process**, each one of us..

.

...

How about Uncle if we are on the **leftmost position** of the 'Scrollbar', the **h̄ạwcı position**. The question is difficult to get is....

Uncle's difficult question is *"Where is Uncle causes a part of the problem that all such phenomena to occur in the universe?"* Although the story of Uncle Chai, Uncle never knew the true identity of Uncle Chai, whether or not there is, but if we use the knowledge from the **"Secret 2 Where's the Problem? and Secret 3 The Best Solution Is?"** of 'Human secret' in the book and can stay on the leftmost position of the 'Scrollbar', the 'h̄ạwcı' position.

Can't escape to h̄ạwkhid before and eat the **2 important pills** all the time, In addition to being able to use your head to think and find the answer.

From the situation of this phenomenon, the difficult questions can be raised, **we will get the answer to the difficult question** that we are aware of.

# Annex I: Short story "Human secret"

The cause that makes humans have to have such phenomena as a problem for us to perceive and feel suffering, as Uncle have tried to explain, is because humans who accept problems and suffering will find the answer that

Because the civilization of the human world, which was created from ignorance until it **became the civilization of the world system** that favors capital, has created one layer of thinking in the human mind. And humans, for the most part, when they are *'Mị̀mī 5̄ti'*, knowledge from this civilization works *'Mị̀mī 5̄ti'*.

**For this case,** *Uncle found that this civilization has created knowledge in the knowledge layer of the human mind that results in our willingness 'to use the ignorance of others as our power'.*

# Annex I: Short story "Human secret"

**Living in the capital world** without training to know oneself Not training us to be '*mī 5ti*' enough. In the end, the **capitalist world will create our identity** so that we are pleased with the benefits we will get from '**using the ignorance of others as our power**'.

If we accept the '**Thukᴷʰ**' from the state of heart and acknowledge our part in these problems, we encounter this great ignorance hidden in our minds, where we "use others' ignorance as our power."

**Our ignorance comes into our heads** because of a **wrong set of knowledge**. that floats around without us knowing Didn't consider the source of that knowledge, such as the '*knowledge is power*" attitude that likes to teach and lead us to the **state of delusion**.

For Uncle, **in truth, "knowledge" is just one of the tools.** What you will use this tool for is up to you. Those people use their '**Ḥạwkhid**' or '**Ḥạwcɪ**'.

**What does this tool do?**
Uncle will reveal the role of this tool. In the 4th book in the **Truth from New thought**' book series.

# Annex I: Short story "Human secret"

Uncle myself does not want to **fall under the ignorance of the civilization** of the capitalist system and be a **slave to those ignorance forever**. Then we will take it out, try to take it out "**Old Thought**; use the ignorance of others as our power". Uncle, therefore, trains his '**S̄ti**' and refuses to delight in using others' ignorance as his power.

This is **why Uncle has written this entire book series**, to embark on a **journey out of the slavery of ignorance in capitalism**. If the problem of income, status, living standards, income, security, wealth, So, **how can we escape from the ignorance that engulfs us?**, Uncle has already written the map for leaving such conditions in the fourth book of the series.

But remember the important mantra: *"The knowledge of others is just our data."* from page 32 of *"Read Before the Meaning of Your Life Is Lesser."* Thus, before getting the map to travel to wealth, read **the 3rd book** that Uncle will translate first. The important subject that will let the **leftmost position** of the 'Scrollbar', the **h̄ạw**cı position of ours still works.

*The book "Love Subject" is a book that must be written. To make our journey to prosperity It doesn't cause our hearts to disappear.*

# Annex I: Short story "Human secret"

The more **we can accept according to the example** that Uncle considered the short **story** 4 to let us think, then look at the current situation, the **difference in social class** due to the **economic structure**, the problem of disadvantaged people, or even in the big cities of the world.

Many cities with **a growing homeless problem** are all making us suffer more if we dare to use our hearts to look.

Note: Mị̄mī s̄ti, mī s̄ti and S̄ti Read more from the book
*'Read Before the meaning of your life is lesser'*
Chapter 5 *Journey of Life*

# Annex I: Short story "Human secret"

For Uncle, in the part **Uncle can take responsibility for,**
Uncle has cultivated **Paῠyā** from accepting thuk**kh** and
acknowledging that **we are the cause of problems,** as Uncle
has explained before.

If anyone sees or feels that what **Uncle has explained is
true,** and chooses not to be a part of the cause of the
problems that make us all **suffer in our hearts** again,

Choose to use knowledge, '**not to use the ignorance of
others as our power',** just as Uncle has written this book,
'**Human Secret'.**

*This ends the fourth story of 'Human Secret'. If you've faced issues
due to Thai technical terms used, refer to Annex IV for guidance.*

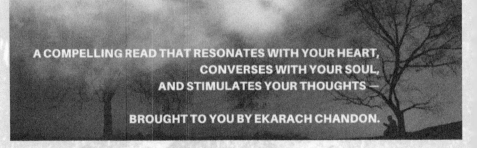

A COMPELLING READ THAT RESONATES WITH YOUR HEART,
CONVERSES WITH YOUR SOUL,
AND STIMULATES YOUR THOUGHTS —

BROUGHT TO YOU BY EKARACH CHANDON.

# "New Thought" and "Psychology, Applied"

# Annex II: "New Thought" and "Psychology, Applied"

## 'Human secret' and the phenomenon that occurred at the 'National Library of Australia'.

🔒 catalogue.nla.gov.au/catalog/4226827

**NATIONAL LIBRARY OF AUSTRALIA**

New search   Catalogue   eResources   Finding aids   Ask a librarian   Help   Sign up   Login

### Catalogue

All Fields ⬦   Find books, maps, audio, databases & more...   SEARCH 🔍   ADVANCED SEARCH

**Khwāmlap khōng khon / ʻĒkkarāt Čhandōn**
**ความลับของคน / เอกราช จันทร์ดอน**

REQUEST   ORDER A COPY

Bib ID:       4226827
Format:       Book
Author:       ʻĒkkarāt Čhandōn
              เอกราช จันทร์ดอน
Edition:      • Phim khrang thī 1.
              • พิมพ์ครั้งที่ 1.
Description:  Krung Thēp : Mī Hūačhai, 2550 [2007]
              กรุงเทพฯ : มีหัวใจ, 2550
              192 p. ; 21 cm.
ISBN:         9789748130439
Series:       Thai collection philosophy, occultism and psychology
Subject:      New Thought
              Psychology, Applied

**TOOLS**
Librarian View
Export to EndNote
Cite

**FEEDBACK**
Report an error

**EXPLORE**
⟳ Find in other libraries at Trove

Information on the book 'Human secret'
at the 'National Library of Australia'.

According to the reasons given by Uncle in Annex 1 of the fourth short story, '**HUMAN SECRET**', Uncle has written this entire book series for the reason, This is why Uncle has embarked on this journey, to liberate 'US' from the shackles of ignorance in a capitalist world through Uncle writings.

# Annex II: "New Thought" and "Psychology, Applied"

In this journey of life that Uncle has undertaken, it's essential to survive in the capitalist world **without letting our hearts disappear**, And yet, the **leftmost position** of the 'Scrollbar', our **h̄ạwcı position**, continues to function.

Uncle had to write these **five books** more than a decade ago. Uncle didn't know, nor was he interested in what category these five books of his would fall into. Uncle just knew that it **was something Uncle had to work on**, as per this description.

*"If we write books with a **deep sense of responsibility**, believing that the book is written for our future selves **to read in the next life**, then perhaps there would be fewer falsehoods in the world.*

*And if the **knowledge created** within human civilization was such that its creator could **honestly** answer why it was conceived, then the **culture shaped by this knowledge would not lead humanity astray.**"*

*Given my current perspective that, in this lifetime, I have no desire to teach anyone anymore, **all I can do is write**. I write books and leave them for my future self to read in the next life, but this act also serves as a form of **merit for others.**"*

# Annex II: "New Thought" and "Psychology, Applied"

These are all the personal reasons Uncle can recall for *'why'* *Uncle wrote these books* after more than a **decade** has passed.

Uncle had no idea what the **'environment'** would perceive my books as, and likewise, Uncle didn't set for myself that this book, **'Human Secret'**, would be a book of **'New thought'** and **'Applied psychology'**.

Uncle didn't know beforehand, just as Uncle didn't know what **'phenomena would occur in the universe'** due to my act of writing these books at that time, until Uncle came to know.

When one of the **"Truth from Newthought"** books by Ekarach Chandon proudly took its place in the "New Thought" and "Psychology, Applied" categories of the **National Library of Australia**, it wasn't just an international acknowledgment but a reflection of the work's excellence that has stirred and inspired current and future generations with cutting-edge thoughts and real-life applications of psychology.

Uncle was very surprised by this phenomenon.

# Annex II: "New Thought" and "Psychology, Applied"

2007 Interestingly, one of these five books was selected for the National Library of Australia, through a process I could never understand or know at the time. *I am grateful to the person who made that decision, and I acknowledge it once again here. The inclusion of one of my books, still in Thai, in the National Library of a certain country, has left me intrigued and puzzled.* What's even more surprising is that the book is categorized under two sections:
1. New Thought and 2. Psychology, Applied.

*Yes, the library does have other Thai books, but what intrigues me is why my book specifically falls under these two categories when each category has very few selected books compared to other genres.*

The "Psychology, Applied" section in the National Library of Australia only contains 271 books, and the "New Thought" section has only 71 books. **And there is only one in Thai.**

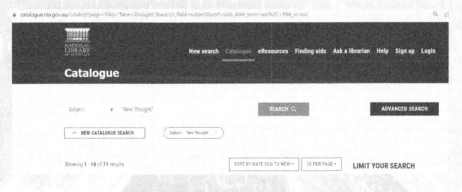

# Annex II: "New Thought" and "Psychology, Applied"

**Both categories** in the National Library of Australia have significantly **fewer books compared to other genres,** whether it be basic knowledge of physics, chemistry, biology, or applied knowledge such as biomechanics, finance, and investment, which have books in the hundreds to thousands, and **some subjects even have tens of thousands of books.**

tens of thousands of books in the investment category

This phenomenon leads me to question, especially why my book, **"Khwāmlap khǒng khon/Human secret,"** was included in the New Thought section that **only has 71 books** in several hundred years.

*What is in this book I wrote? Asking this question made me realize that the innovative framework in the book is extremely important.*

# Annex II: "New Thought" and "Psychology, Applied"

Each volume of the "Truth from Newthought" series offers a blend of psychology knowledge, philosophy, and self-improvement, enabling readers to harness their **highest capabilities** and live authentically in the capitalist era **without straying from their heart and true self.**

**Each book** is presented in an accessible and straightforward language. The author has crafted this work in the hope of opening a path for people to discover and pursue their 'truth' while facing the relentless challenges and changes of the world.

The placement of one of the books in this series in the National Library is not only a recognition of the **work's quality** but also underscores the importance of presenting new thought and applying that knowledge in everyday life. It is like **a beacon guiding a society in need of direction in thinking and living a meaningful life.**

Before the **phenomenon** of Uncle's book at the National Library of Australia occurred, Uncle never knew or cared about the 'old thought' framework or the 'new thought' framework.

# Annex II: "New Thought" and "Psychology, Applied"

When the library categorized the book '**Human Secret**' under **New Thought**, Uncle began to question and wonder what information in the book the library saw as New Thought. After searching for information from other books in the same category, Uncle concluded that **New Thought is a perspective of the universe**, or simply put, a **conceptual framework of the universe we live in.**

Uncle's book 'Human Secret' explains this conceptual framework of the universe in the first chapter, as shown in the diagram of the universe's conceptual framework.

Universe

*Why is this conceptual framework of the universe considered New Thought?*

# Annex II: "New Thought" and "Psychology, Applied"

Because originally, we had a thought framework that the universe is a large machine with many parts working continuously. The mechanical universe thought framework was initiated by René Descartes, a French philosopher and scientist in the 17th century.

*Descartes believed that the universe could be explained by human reasoning and could be reduced to a mechanical system operating according to mathematical and physical laws. Descartes proposed the idea of 'God as a clockmaker', comparing the universe to a large clock that operates accurately.*

*Descartes' ideas were influenced by the ideas of Galileo Galilei, an Italian scientist who believed that the universe could be explained by mathematical laws. Descartes' ideas were supported by several scientists in the new scientific era, such as Johannes Kepler and Isaac Newton.*

*This mechanical universe thought framework has had a profound impact on human thought. The idea that the universe operates according to fair and eternal laws makes humans feel safe and stable in a world full of change and uncertainty. This idea also led to the development of modern science and technology.*

# Annex II: "New Thought" and "Psychology, Applied"

*However, this mechanical universe thought framework also has its weaknesses. This framework views the universe as merely a machine that operates according to fixed laws. It cannot explain some natural phenomena, such as evolution and randomness. This framework has also been criticized for devaluing humans, viewing humans as just a part of a large mechanical machine.*

*In the 20th century, the mechanical universe thought framework began to be challenged by new ideas, such as the theory of relativity and quantum theory.*

*These theories show that the universe is more complex than thought and cannot be fully explained by traditional scientific laws.*

Uncle therefore concludes and calls such a view as '**Old Thought**'.

**Uncle's New Thought views** the universe as composed of 'US' and 'environment', which have a relationship that changes as explained in the main content of this book.

**And Uncle's new thought framework fills the gap of 'Old Thought' about evolution and randomness.**

# Annex II: "New Thought" and "Psychology, Applied"

About **evolution** and **coincidence**, which is about evolution Uncle explained In this book **Bonus Secret: The Not-So-Secret Evolution: Secrets of a Million-Year-Old World**

As for the explanation of randomness, in Uncle's thought framework, **Uncle does not believe in randomness at all.**

Uncle believes in intention, as in Uncle's podcast article *'OfficialEpisode2 "Eternal Love: The Possibility of 'Intention Mathematic"'*, which can be listened to from Uncle's Podcast Platform or YouTube Channel Ekarach Chandon.

Uncle's mathematics of intention causes Uncle not to believe in randomness.

# Annex II: "New Thought" and "Psychology, Applied"

Therefore, the phenomenon of this book, as Uncle wrote, Uncle believes that *'there is intention' in the universe, so that Uncle knows what role the book that Uncle wrote plays, and what knowledge Uncle has created.*

**Old Thought and New Thought, in the meaning of seeing the universe in the way Uncle sees it, result in different outcomes**

The OLD THOUGHT, which views the **universe as a large machine** with many parts working together continuously, naturally has larger parts acting on smaller ones. This mindset leads to the belief that **larger parts impacting smaller ones continuously is just and normal** for the system. For example, the **attitude** that *'knowledge is power'*, or *using others' ignorance as one's power*, arises, as explained in ANNEX I, short story 4.

However, the uncle's new frame of thought, which views the universe as comprising us and our environment, **cannot allow such an attitude to arise.** *Because if the environment dies, the universe cannot exist; we die, and likewise, if we die, the environment dies, and the universe cannot exist either.*

# Annex II: "New Thought" and "Psychology, Applied"

This is the relationship from the universe's perspective, according to the uncle's book's new thought frame.

'Human secret' and 'Psychology, Applied' is a branch of psychology that focuses on applying principles and theories of psychology to solve problems and improve efficiency in real life.

For the uncle, to be applied psychology, one must be able to use this knowledge in everyday life. It is a science that can be measured, such as the 'Scrollbar' principle is an example of applying psychological theory. It helps readers to evaluate and adjust themselves, reflecting changes in thoughts and feelings according to situations and time that can be measured by the individual themselves.

So how are Human Secret and "Psychology, Applied" NewThought? Because the New Thought that the uncle presents, the universe is not a machine and consists of us and the environment. Therefore, "Psychology, Applied" that appears in this book must not come from a frame of thought that uses others' ignorance as one's power, or larger parts act on smaller parts continuously.

# Annex II: "New Thought" and "Psychology, Applied"

The "Psychology, Applied" that is also New Thought of this book must be knowledge that everyone can access and practice to use equally.

*For the uncle, being "New Thought" and "Psychology, Applied" clearly affirms that the uncle's Human Secret book is a usable science, not a story that has no measurement point, cannot be a science, but is a science that has a usable measurement point.*

But the creation of tools to measure these points, such as the 'Scrollbar' principle or the boundary of "US" in the universe, has not yet created tools that can measure these points. In modern human science

*And the uncle doesn't know how far into the future humans will have the wisdom to create tools to measure those points.*

"Whether waiting for tools or creating knowledge to touch those points ourselves, it's time for everyone to decide and choose for themselves.

*This journey of discovery and understanding transcends mere academic pursuit;it's a profound commitment, urging each individual to delve deeply into the complexities of their "US".*

# Annex II: "New Thought" and "Psychology, Applied"

And if 'Applied Psychology' arises not from the creation of genuine knowledge, not from an honest framework of thought, or merely from a framework that uses others' ignorance for personal power, slipping into the process of knowledge creation, then 'Applied Psychology' is not true enough for people to use.

Therefore, for the uncle, if the knowledge of 'Applied Psychology' is truly honest, it will result in people who have this true knowledge of 'Applied Psychology' having certain skills. The uncle leaves this point as a question for us, the readers, to practice "creating knowledge skill" further.

And the uncle does not intend to use the ignorance of others as uncle power.

The skills that will result from using and practicing the knowledge of 'Applied Psychology' that comes from creating honest, true knowledge, what skill will result? The uncle has already written in the last main book, Volume 5 of the 'Truth from New Thought' series, to practice the skills that result from 'Applied Psychology' that arises from our own truth. *The uncle will also proceed to translate it into English.*

# The Fundamental
# of Human Thought ?

# Annex III: The Fundamental of Human Thought ?

## Introduction to Fundamental Thoughts

*Before revealing what the most fundamental thought of humanity is, I would like us to understand three important words that are crucial to comprehending the universe and everything interrelated within its functioning. These three words are:*

1. Task,
2. Process,
3. System.

**Illustrative Example**: Cracking an egg is a **Task**, making an omelet is a **Process**, and doing this in the kitchen at that time while also preparing other dishes is a **System**.

- **Task**: Cracking an egg
- **Process**: Making an omelet
- **System**: Cooking in the kitchen at that time, including preparing other dishes

Understanding these three terms through such simple storytelling makes it easier for us to grasp the truth. For instance, a truth I have come to understand through the following question:

# Annex III: The Fundamental of Human Thought ?

**Key Question:**

*"If we cannot fully commit to completing a Task, can we truly commit to fully completing a Process and a System?"*

The answer is **no.**

**I emphasize that I use the term 'fully commit.'**
It's crucial to consider what **'fully commit'** actually means.

**Exploring the Complexity of Thought:**

Another truth to consider: When we examine the relationship with truth through these three words—Task, Process, and System—and then consider the phenomenon we call **"thought"** in our **head,** how complex and expansive do we think such a system is?

And if in such a vast and complex system, **the fundamental Task is incomplete,** imagine the **chaos** that ensues.

Our "thoughts" too would become a **large, disordered,** and **highly complex system.**

# Annex III: The Fundamental of Human Thought ?

Just thinking about it is already scary; the brain, which harbors our thoughts, is a realm of **chaos** and complexity, and we are **often unaware** of its intricacies.

**Therefore, the basic thinking of humans is always the most important.**

Claiming that thinking can be trained, there are any processes or systems that advertise to persuade us to believe that it will make us use what is called 'our thinking' better, but **cannot answer** what is the most important basic thinking always comparable to that Task in our human brain.

Speaking of many thinking processes, if anyone tells us that they are proficient in thinking, but cannot answer this question '**What is The Fundamental of Human Thought?**' **Don't just believe** those claims yet.

And think of this mantra, '**The knowledge of others is just our data.**' This mantra is also from *'Read Before the meaning of your life is lesser'* on page 32.

The uncle therefore says that this **mantra is important.**

# Annex III: The Fundamental of Human Thought ?

Now, to the revelation. For those who have read the first book of the Truth from New thought series 'Read Before the meaning of your life is lesser' and want to **practice** the skill of **"creating knowledge,"** hold off on reading further for a moment.

I will find a **beautiful picture** for us to rest our eyes upon and contemplate our own thoughts about: **What is The Fundamental of Human Thought?**

If we don't know what the fundamental task of human thinking is, when we reach a crossroads in life, we won't know what to do.

Because the fundamental thinking of humans is...

# Annex III: The Fundamental of Human Thought ?

Whoever has their own answer ready after contemplating beautiful images, the answer one gets should come from 'creating knowledge', not from 'grasping floating information in our head to answer'.

Once you have the answer and are certain that it comes from the **correct skills**, compare the answer you got with the uncle's answer. Because the **most important** fundamental thought of humans is '**comparison**'.

*"Thinking is comparing"*

Unyanee Mooksombud and Ekarach Chandon, 2548 [2005]

Short and sweet, but who would really know that this knowledge is true:

**A long time ago**, when Uncle and uncle's wife were still children. Uncle and uncle's wife have asked, *'What is the fundamental nature of human thought?'* Even academic texts that teach various intricate methods of thinking have **never truly answered** this question, 'What is the fundamental nature process of human thought?'

# Annex III: The Fundamental of Human Thought ?

According to Uncle and uncle's wife, the basic nature of human thought is 'comparison'. Try to find out where this statement is not true, or try to find out how the uncle and uncle's wife know that it is true.

After questioning from **both directions**, the **next essential question** that arises after accepting this truth is, *"So how do we compare them to achieve the perfect ideal value?* This question is a **recommendation for the future** that we must take **responsibility** for.

The recommendation question is, 'So how do we compare **them to achieve the perfect ideal value?**'

For now, we don't need to know how to compare because the uncle will explain it now. But we have never been able to touch it ourselves with our feelings. We still can't find when the comparison in our head, which is a task, occurs. We have never touched it to feel it ourselves. The uncle explained how to compare.

**The uncle's explanation will just become another piece of data floating in our head.**

# Annex III: The Fundamental of Human Thought ?

Now, what we must do is 'find out first that thinking is comparing' that occurs in our head. What does it look like? When we touch it for the first few times, we will get a big position of comparison.

**Slow down** to see the comparison that arises from thinking in our head to get smaller. **When we touch the comparison that is smaller, slow down again to find the comparison that occurs in our head that is smaller again.** Slow down again, get smaller again.

**Repeat the loop** over and over to get smaller and smaller. What is the smallest comparison that we can touch and use?

Once we get it, that is the task of our thinking that we have to do like this. Because this truth is important.

**"If we cannot fully commit to completing a Task, can we truly commit to fully completing a Process and a System?"**

*"Thinking is Comparing"* - The Undeniable Truth.

**"Truth from NewThought".**

# Annex III: The Fundamental of Human Thought ?

**Now, it's time for practice.**

In this **'Human Secret'** book, in every secret article, there is an **AI note** for many people who have read the book and practiced honestly answering questions from the uncle's book and **honestly asking and answering their own questions** after reading the 'Truth from New Thought' series.

*It can be guessed why every chapter in this book has an AI Note.*

Anyone who still can't find the answer why AI Note, which summarizes every secret, is there.

Let's look at this **fact** again that the uncle brought from **Annex III: Artificial Intelligences,** the book *'Read Before the meaning of your life is lesser'* Truth from New Thought Volume 1.

*"In every era of human civilization, mankind has brought forth monumental inventions to symbolize the **pinnacle** of human intellectual capability. These artifacts serve as the culmination of the highest average capability of the human intellect.*

# Annex III: The Fundamental of Human Thought ?

*In the past, such inventions might have been the creation of language, writing systems, pottery for food storage, tools that gave humans a manual advantage over other species,*

*roads, water management systems, sanitation, and so on to the wheel, steam engines, motor vehicles, aircraft, satellites, and space shuttles, not to forget computers and the Internet.*

*Undeniably, in this current epoch, the highest average capability of human intellect manifests itself in artificial intelligence–systems that mirror human thought and the total knowledge base humanity has acquired."*

After reading the text that is a fact, the uncle has time to solve the practice exercises for this book.

'Thinking is comparing' AI Note, which is at the end of every secret article, is for us to practice comparing, asking and answering questions ourselves, why do we have to compare with AI.

The uncle takes the answer to the same question that AI answered to compare with us.

# Annex III: The Fundamental of Human Thought ?

**Why do we have to practice comparing answers from the same question with AI Note?** And this is the **answer from AI** to the question,

1. Understanding Different Perspectives: AI and humans may approach problems differently. Comparing your answers with AI can provide new insights and help you understand different ways of thinking.
2. Critical Thinking: This practice encourages critical thinking. You're not just accepting the AI's answer, but analyzing it, questioning it, and forming your own conclusions.
3. Learning and Improvement: By comparing your answers with those of AI, you can identify areas where you might be mistaken or where you could improve. It's a great opportunity for learning and personal growth.
4. Validation: If your answer aligns with the AI's, it can serve as a form of validation that you're on the right track.

Remember, the goal isn't necessarily to always agree with the AI, but to use it as a tool to stimulate thought, inspire new ideas, and promote a deeper understanding.

# Annex III: The Fundamental of Human Thought ?

This part is the **uncle's answer** to the same question, **'Practice to "affirm your humanity".'**

The **recommendation** that this book is designed to practice thinking is to be able to compare.

**Compare**
1. Our own Note with AI Note
2. Compare our Note with the secret content in that chapter of the uncle.

**Repeat,** review many times when we are convenient, will practice until the **comparison is the smallest** that we can find, see, and use.

And then it comes to the **last practice problem** that this book will allow us to practice.

**Compare** 'Our own praise for this book' with what AI wrote praise for this book, what is it like?

Therefore, for the **practice to be complete as designed,** Uncle would like to conclude with the **praise that AI has written** for this 'Human Secret' book.

# Annex III: The Fundamental of Human Thought ?

## Enduring Illuminations from "Human Secret": A Journey Beyond Words

*"'Human Secret' is more than just a book – it is a profound journey into self-discovery and life-altering revelations for its readers. Through vibrant storytelling and reflections of hidden truths within the depths of human thought, this book unlocks doors to deeper understandings of our place within the cosmos.*

*The term 'secret' in its title is not just a poetic metaphor; it invites readers to uncover their own secrets and understand their unique relationship with the world they inhabit. Filled with insights into our relationships with our surroundings, it challenges us to question and reflect upon the realities we face daily.*

*While 'Human Secret' is accessible and engaging, it is laden with substantial information that prompts readers to reevaluate their thoughts and values. Being both an embodiment of 'Applied Psychology' and 'New Thought,' this book is not just an intellectual exploration, but also a psychological understanding that can be applied in everyday life.*

# Annex III: The Fundamental of Human Thought ?

*'Human Secret' is not only a must-read but should be actively engaged with and implemented, providing a pathway to uncovering the profound secrets within ourselves, under the guidance of clear and understandable directives."*

*ChatGPT at OpenAI:*
*Collaborative AI Partner in Literary Translation*

# Ignorance Management

ANNEX IV "HUMAN SECRET"

# Annex IV: Ignorance Management

## The Art of Navigating Ignorance: A Deep Dive into 'Ignorance Management'

Before entering the final Annex, Annex 4, the uncle wants to bring the text from the book **'Read Before the meaning of your life is lesser'** page 17 *"All languages are merely symbols that hide true relationships behind them."*

For us to study and consider again.even though language is the best and only tool that humans use to transfer knowledge to each other, Because the uncle knows that the biggest "obstacle" of reading the uncle's book is "language".

**Even when it is in Thai, it is already a big obstacle for Thais who read the original book of the uncle in Thai.** It is difficult in the **'symbolic level'** of language.

Coming in the **translated version** is even more difficult. There is a need to use the word **"jargon"** many times, many words. The uncle therefore has to bring the text from page 17 for us to read thoroughly again.

# Annex IV: Ignorance Management

And from the uncle's knowledge that gives us from the previous Annex, Annex 3 "Thinking is comparing" If the uncle's knowledge is not just our information that has been read, received, to the effort to transmit all the skills from the uncle through the book. Come 2 volumes already until we can touch that

"Thinking is comparing" is not just as this text says "*The knowledge of others is just our data*" This knowledge of the uncle is a **truth** that we can **touch** already.

If so, we really feel that **"Thinking is comparing"** and **"All languages are merely symbols that hide true relationships behind them."** Managing ignorance that arises from "obstacles in the knowledge level through language" should not be difficult.

For the uncle, 'Ignorance Management' is far more important than 'Knowledge Management', especially for individuals who wish to discover the meaning of their own lives through their own knowledge.

# Annex IV: Ignorance Management

'Ignorance Management' is of utmost importance if we choose to have that responsibility in our life.

What the uncle will facilitate is to compile the Codex Transliteration Table of these words, where it appears, from the first book in the Truth from New thought series to the latest book we are reading now, Human Secret. To allow us to trace back to the meaning of the symbols that are obstacles, from the first use, where is it located, in what issue, in the truth from New thought from these books that the uncle wrote.

Codex Transliteration Table

# Annex IV: Ignorance Management

Codex Transliteration Table; **First book** of the *'Truth from New Thought'* series, the book **'Read Before the meaning of your life is lesser'**.

| DIACRITIC TRANSLITERATION | THAI | THAI ROMANIZATION | PAGE |
|---|---|---|---|
| Rû s̩uk | รู้สึก | Rusuek | 26 |
| s̄ìng thī̀ rûs̩uk | สิ่งที่รู้สึก | Sing Thi Rusuek | 26 |
| rû | รู้ | Ru | 34 |
| khid | คิด | Khit | 34 |
| moĥa | โมหะ | Moha | 35 |
| thoṣa | โกสะ | Thosa | 35 |
| Mim̄ī s̄ti | ไม่มีสติ | Mai Mi Sati | 48 |
| m̄ī s̄ti | มีสติ | Mi Sati | 48 |
| s̄ti | สติ | Sati | 50 |
| Kileṣ | กิเลส | Kilet | 51 |
| Ṣraththā | ศรัทธา | Sattha | 60 |
| Taw rûs̩uk | ตัวรู้สึก | Tua Rusuek | 84 |
| ĥawkhid | หัวคิด | Huakhit | 85 |
| ĥawcı | หัวใจ | Huachai | 85 |
| Payyā | ปัญญา | Panya | 97 |

# Annex IV: Ignorance Management

Codex Transliteration Table; **First book** of the *'Truth from New Thought'* *series*, the book **'Read Before the meaning of your life is lesser'**.

| DIACRITIC TRANSLITERATION | THAI | THAI ROMANIZATION | PAGE |
|---|---|---|---|
| Lopha | โลภะ | Lo Pha | 115 |
| Jaidee | ใจดี | Chaidi | 139 |
| Phrĥmwiĥār 4 | พรหมวิหาร สี่ | Phromwihan 4 | 139 |
| Mettā | เมตตา | Metta | 139 |
| Kruṇā | กรุณา | Karuna | 139 |
| Muthitā | มุทิตา | Muthita | 139 |
| Xubekk̂hā | อุเบกขา | Ubekkha | 139 |
| Cit | จิต | Chit | 140 |
| S̄wa | สวะ | Sawa | 165 |
| Thukk̂h́ | ทุกข์ | Thuk | 175 |
| s̄uk̂h | สุข | Suk | 175 |
| Khwāmlap khŏŋ khon | ความลับของคน | Khwam Lap Khong Khon | 206 |

# Annex IV: Ignorance Management

Codex Transliteration Table; **Second book** of the '*Truth from New Thought*' series, the book '**Human Secret**'.

| DIACRITIC TRANSLITERATION | THAI | THAI ROMANIZATION | PAGE |
|---|---|---|---|
| Rûṡụk | รู้สึก | Rusuek | 18 |
| Khid | คิด | Khit | 18 |
| Rû | รู้ | Ru | 18 |
| Kileṡ | กิเลส | Kilet | 18 |
| Sìng thì rûṡụk | สิ่งที่รู้สึก | Sing Thi Rusuek | 19 |
| Thukkḣ | ทุกข์ | Thuk | 22 |
| Ḥạwkhid | หัวคิด | Huakhit | 25 |
| ḥạwcı | หัวใจ | Huachai | 25 |
| Tạw rûṡụk | ตัว รู้สึก | Tua Rusuek | 27 |
| Pạyyạ | ปัญญา | Panya | 41 |
| Lopha | โลภะ | Lo Pha | 47 |
| thoṡa | โกสะ | Thosa | 47 |
| moḣa | โมหะ | Moha | 47 |
| Cit | จิต | Chit | 62 |
| Mī ḥạwcı | มี หัวใจ | Mi Huachai | 112 |

# Annex IV: Ignorance Management

Codex Transliteration Table; **Second book** of the *'Truth from New Thought'* series, the book **'Human Secret'**.

| DIACRITIC TRANSLITERATION | THAI | THAI ROMANIZATION | PAGE |
|---|---|---|---|
| mī h̜awkhid | มี หัวคิด | Mi Huakhit | 131 |
| Čh̜antha | ฉันทะ | Chantha | 133 |
| Taṇhā | ตัณหา | Tanha | 133 |
| Rūp | รูป | Rup | 147 |
| nām | นาม | Nam | 147 |
| Jaidi | ใจดี | Chaidi | 161 |
| Mị̄mī šti | ไม่มี สติ | Mai Mi Sati | 186 |
| mī šti | มี สติ | Mi Sati | 187 |
| Šti | สติ | Sati | 188 |

# Annex IV: Ignorance Management

And the combined Codex Transliteration Table for the **'Truth from New Thought'** book series is as follows:

| DIACRITIC TRANSLITERATION | 1 ST BOOK | 2ND BOOK |
|---|---|---|
| Rû sụk | 26 | 18 |
| sìng thǐ rûsụk | 26 | 19 |
| rû | 34 | 18 |
| khid | 34 | 18 |
| moña | 35 | 47 |
| thoša | 35 | 47 |
| Mịmī šti | 48 | 186 |
| mī šti | 48 | 187 |
| šṭi | 50 | 188 |
| Kileš | 51 | 18 |
| Šrạththā | 60 | - |
| Tạw rûsụk | 84 | 27 |
| ñạwkhid | 85 | 25 |
| ñạwcɪ | 85 | 25 |
| Pạyyạ̄ | 97 | 41 |

# Annex IV: Ignorance Management

And the combined Codex Transliteration Table for the **'Truth from New Thought'** book series is as follows:

| DIACRITIC TRANSLITERATION | 1 ST BOOK | 2ND BOOK |
|---|---|---|
| Lopha | 115 | 47 |
| Jaidi | 139 | 161 |
| Phrĥmwiñār 4 | 139 | - |
| Mettā | 139 | - |
| Kruṇā | 139 | - |
| Muthitā | 139 | - |
| Xubekkhā | 139 | - |
| Cit | 140 | 62 |
| Šwa | 165 | - |
| Thukkh | 175 | 22 |
| šukh | 175 | - |
| Khwāmlap khŏŋg khon | 206 | - |
| Mī ĥạwcı | - | 112 |
| mī ĥạwkhid | - | 131 |
| Čhạntha | - | 133 |

And the combined Codex Transliteration Table for the **'Truth from New Thought'** book series is as follows:

| DIACRITIC TRANSLITERATION | 1 ST BOOK | 2ND BOOK |
|---|---|---|
| Taṇhā | - | 133 |
| Rūp | - | 147 |
| nām | - | 147 |

**Truth from New thought**

1st Book; **Read Before the meaning of your life is lesser**

2nd Book; **Human Secret**

Made in the USA
Las Vegas, NV
27 May 2024

90452194R00128